THE STRUGGLES
That Bring Joy

Austin-Romaine D. Mahoney

PREFACE

In delving into the captivating narrative of Joseph's life as depicted in the Bible, I found myself pondering the intricacies of his journey and the adversities that marked his path. Little did I grasp that, much like Joseph, my own struggles were not mere happenstance but rather the shaping tools employed by the divine hand of God, molding the essence of the person God intended me to become.

Joseph's narrative unfolds against a backdrop of trials and tribulations, yet through these challenges, he emerges as a leader destined to guide a nation. It is a realization that echoes with profound significance in my own life. No longer do I question the reasons behind Joseph's seemingly harsh ordeals; instead, I am on the verge of understanding. For Joseph, joy sprouted from the very trials that seemed to be his undoing.

Reflecting on this parallel, I recognize that, akin to Joseph's preparation as a devoted disciple, my own trials have been the chisel shaping my character. Just as Joseph was primed to fulfill God's will and nourish a nation, I, too, have been honed by adversity to share a meaningful repast with my fellow citizens, contributing to the elevation of our collective society. The journey is not merely a solitary endeavor but a preparation for a greater purpose—a purpose woven into the fabric of a larger narrative where trials are not stumbling blocks but steppingstones toward a fulfilling and purposeful life.

ACKNOWLEDGMENTS

I want to acknowledge Jesus Christ as the Lord and Savior of my life. Having hope and being led by the Holy Spirit motivated me to write and tell you, my story. I want to thank my son, Micah Mahoney. My son changed my viewpoint for the better; he is why I am on this journey today. Micah pushed me every day to give life one hundred percent instead of eighty percent, he drives me to be persistent, and his beautiful smile motivates me daily to keep writing. Finally, I would like to thank my mother, sister, brother, and everyone who edited and pre-read my book before it was published.

INTRODUCTION

Let me take you on a journey through the pages of "The Struggles That Bring Joy," where the narrative unfolds as a tapestry woven from real-life experiences, triumphs over barriers, and the overcoming of fears. Picture life as a vast garden—lush and vibrant, dotted with dead leaves, unruly weeds, and flowers that need careful tending. Much like our lives, this garden holds the potential for both decay and blossoming beauty. The metaphorical dead leaves and bad mulches symbolize the hurdles and challenges we encounter. When neglected, the garden's flowers wither, and the vibrant hummingbirds and butterflies disappear.

Yet, in the midst of this analogy lies a profound truth—a truth that forms the essence of this narrative. A transformation occurs if we pause to care for our metaphorical garden, meticulously weeding out negativity, mulching the soil, and nurturing the plants. Not only do butterflies and hummingbirds return, but an entire ecosystem of joy, peace, and happiness emerges. Bees and other delightful creatures become symbolic manifestations of the joy cultivated within. The metaphor extends to the pursuit of happiness itself. Chasing butterflies, much like chasing happiness, becomes an endless endeavor if not grounded in the fundamental care of one's garden—of oneself. The encouragement here is not to pursue ephemeral joys but to focus inward, to tend to the garden of the soul.

This book is a motivational compass, guiding you to pay attention to your surroundings and internal landscape. It calls for belief in yourself, in your capacity to cultivate a garden where the flowers of happiness, joy, and peace bloom and thrive. So, let us embark on this journey together, learning to remove the dead leaves, fertilize the soil, and mulch the garden bed of our lives, ushering in a season of blossoming and attracting the abundance of happiness that awaits.

Contents

THE STRUGGLES THAT BRING JOY

I was born and raised by a single parent,
Poverty and crime were the only love I could have inherited,
Now there are six of us in one room that is how we share it,
I have seen dead bodies for days after days. That is why death...I never fear it.
Where was my dad when I needed him?
I heard he is a gangster in the streets, but I have never seen him,
it is like I am living to die, or I am just dreaming,
Looking at myself in the mirror, I know I will never be him.
Can you hear me now!!!?
Or I should say do you fear me now?
I am much older, so you cannot declare me now,
I am just a kid trying to make it through life anyhow.

GROWING UP AS A CHILD

One of the most challenging things for me was getting out of bed in the morning or the feeling of not getting out of bed at all. Not that I slept on a king-size bed or one of Hollywood's massive California beds, which were brimming with wonders and dreams. I was lying on the sponge. The sponge was riddled with holes, and, on rare occasions, it had hair from other people who had slept on it. Let us just say the sponge I am referring to is a generational mattress passed down from one family member to the next.

The best part of sleeping on the sponge is that it was passed down to me by my older brother Antonio, who has since moved to sleep on the living room couch. I am glad not to sleep on the floor like my cousins or the rest of the family. I consider sleeping on the sponge as a special treatment. I want to sleep on the sofa like my elder brother Antonio one day without being yelled at, but for now, I will take the comfort of lying on the sponge. We now have six of us sharing one of the bedrooms in the house. The guys shared one bed, while the girls shared the other. "Move over, man, and don't shake your feet!" As my feet trembled on the bed like a virgin on her wedding night, Anthony, my cousin, yelled, "But I cannot stay still; I just cannot. I must rock a little before bed. Rocking brings me peace; the least I can do to feel happy is rock my feet on a hungry stomach going to bed. Plus, fighting the need to shake my foot would leave me uncomfortable for the rest of the night until I fell asleep. I must shake my legs to become comfortable before I can sleep."

There were only five bedrooms, and it sometimes felt like we were a sausage on a sandwich living together. My uncle slept downstairs in the cellar, my cousins and I slept in the far back near the veranda facing the kitchen, my auntie and uncle shared one room, and my other aunt slept closer to the master bedroom where my grandfather slept. We were considerably luckier than most of the people in our neighborhoods as middle-class families.

My grandfather Mack only had three male grandchildren; my older brother Antonio, my older cousin Anthony, and I are the three boys. The rest of his grandchildren were all females. My grandfather had a total of five children and eleven grandkids. My mother, Joan, my two aunts, Jasmine, and Shelia, and my two uncles, Ryan, and Jordan. It was said that my grandfather has more kids outside the family, but I have never met or heard him talk about them.

My mother, Joan, was the family's eldest of his children. Being the oldest child in a family can sound like a pretty good gig in theory: You're given a few younger siblings you can boss around whenever you want, you can pull the seniority card as needed, and you get the bonus of knowing you had at least one year where you were given every single bit of attention your parents had. Sure, there are positives, but there are also many negatives. There were a few good times with her siblings, but the troubled times outweighed the good. Therefore, she never lived with us because of animosity between her brother and sister. As soon as she was old enough to move out, she went to live with my Stepfather in Mandeville, New Forest, two hours north of St. Elizabeth, Fyyes Pen, where I lived.

Master Hesse, one of our next-door neighbors, was a broom manufacturer. He made excellent stick brooms from cedar trees and thatch. As a result, he had been employed throughout the town and around the island; he was well known for his crafty work. He owned and operated a small shop under the mango tree near his home, and he could often be seen dexterously manipulating straw and stick until his finished creation stood before him. However, making brooms did not put that much money into his pocket. It was a battle for him to make a living, while he had to raise fourteen kids and pay his medical fees. He shared a one-bedroom apartment with a family of fourteen. They did not have the same opportunities as my family. They used the restroom outside and cooked dinner over a wood fire on the rocks. When they did not have anything to eat, sometimes my grandfather would give them a few dollars or prepare a warm meal for them.

Even though it was not much, they appreciated it since anything was better than nothing.

The only times I would see Hesse was on my way to and from school in the mornings and evenings. He would always sit on the stool under the huge mango tree, cutting the broom and getting ready for market with his machete while carving the brooms and getting them ready for market. One morning, I walked past the big mango tree and noticed he was not there, so I asked my grandfather whether or not he had seen Hesse. He replied in a grief-filled voice, "Bwoy, Hesse is sick, and I'm not sure if he'll make it," he added.

"What's the matter with him, and why are you so unsure whether he'll make it?" I asked.

He replied, "The doctor is unsure of his sickness. They think his illness is related to old age, so they put him on bed rest and hope he will get better."

He was dying. I knew he was dying, but why? I asked myself. He used to smile every morning when I would pass by and greet him under the mango tree, and he always seemed unfazed. So, what could have changed? What could have happened within twenty-four hours such that he is now lying on bed rest?

Now, who will I greet in the morning, and who will I look forward to seeing when I get home from school beneath the mango tree? I suppose no one. I am sure his grandkids were more saddened by their grandfather's ailing condition. Everyone in the community knew he was the family's breadwinner. Now, who would provide for his grandkids knowing that the mother is disabled, and the father is no longer in their lives?

I suppose my life was not as awful as I had imagined. If I were ever to compare myself to Hesse's grandchildren, I would have been seen as a wonderful man in their eyes. After a few weeks, it was announced that he had passed away. My grandfather and elders in the community helped dig his grave for burial. His funeral was one of the community's largest I have ever seen. He was one of the poorest men, but had a big heart and was loved by everyone. After his burial, his grandchildren decided to move to Montego Bay, where they could receive more assistance from other relatives.

My grandmother worked as a nurse in the United States, my great-grandfather worked as an electrician and architect in the United Kingdom, my grandfather was a tiler, my uncles were handy, and my mother worked as a travel agent. In contrast, her sisters worked as store clerks. My family had a lot of money coming in from various sources. In my opinion, the financial situation was relatively steady. On the other hand, my grandfather had a serious drinking problem, my uncle Jordan had a gambling problem, my mother did not know how to manage her money, my aunts were shopaholics, and my uncle Ryan was a womanizer. So, the money came in, and quickly went out; therefore, most of our bills were difficult to pay. There was never food in the fridge nor groceries in the cabinet for more than three days. Because the bill was never paid, Jamaica Public Service would continually come and turn off the electricity. It was a good thing we never had to worry about getting our water turned off since the community provided water at the central pipe. Despite our family's wealth, it was still tough to maintain a steady lifestyle, but we thanked God for nature. I would dig yams in the mountains or climb a mango tree to pick fruit when it was in season to relieve my hunger.

Most nights, I would go to bed hungry. Still, the hunger did not bother me on certain nights because I was so accustomed to it that I would just do my homework and go to bed. At times, I would think of my mother and then cry myself to sleep because I missed her. My brother and I would only see her once every two months or whenever my mother could afford our transportation to travel to see her. I enjoyed going to see my mother and spending time with her. She lived with my Stepfather, Paul.

Paul did not do anything around the house. He believed in old traditional love where the woman was supposed to cook, wash, clean, and be submissive to a man. In contrast, the man was to remain brave, loyal, and courageous, uplifting the family. He was neither brave nor courageous, much less loyal. When he arrived home from work, he expected his meal to be ready, the house to be spotless, and his clothing for the next day to be laundered and clean. I was not too fond of how he treated my mother, primarily when he acted like a king in a palace sitting on a high throne. The only thing missing for her was to roll out the red carpet for him. He was miserable and thought highly of himself. My mother did not let it bother her because she did what was necessary to help send my brother and me to school since she was not working. Paul knew my mother depended on him, especially since our father was never in our life. At times he would be genuine and express himself to us as if he cared; however, I could see right through his deceiving ways, that he was using my mother based on her condition. She would always tell him the tables would turn one day and she would no longer need him, but all he would do was laugh at her.

Growing up, I was not my mother's favorite. She showed more interest in my older brother than she would show to me. He had a phone before he was nine years old, was always in the latest sneakers, would get front-seat appearances when we traveled, and was always by her side when she was gossiping about others and telling him fairytale jokes. She favored my older brother above me, and I was constantly called "the stone the builder refused.' One night my mother was ironing and preparing our school uniforms. She did not have an iron board, so she used the side of the bed to iron on. I was playing on the bed, doing backflips, and jumping frogs.

I did a backflip and my left hand landed right on the iron. I cried out for help, but before I knew it, she grabbed me by the throat, said I told you not to jump on the bed and started beating me with a belt on top of my burning hand before taking me to the hospital. She glared at me for six months before I was able to return to her good side. Instead of showing a little sympathy, she only complained about how much money she spent on medical bills that night. The burnt mark remained on my hand for years, and every time I looked at it, it told me that I was merely a stone required if the builder considered me necessary for his project.

My father, well, I have no idea where he was. I did not even have an image of him in my head. I could only think of what I had heard about him, and from what my mother and friends talked about, I knew he was not a man of valor. He was a don, a gangster in the streets, and was a well-known criminal and thug by law enforcement and his enemies. I heard he was on the run and hiding out in trees because his enemies tried to take his life. My father became connected with Christopher Coke, widely known as the Don of the Shower Posses gang, in the late 1980s and early 2000s. During this time, Christopher Coke grew his gang by using firearms, illegal drugs, and other illegal activities sanctioned by the Jamaican Labor Party (JLP). In exchange for the JLP's assistance in the form of ammunition and access to the airport and border so that he could ship guns and cocaine from Colombia and other well-known areas such as Honduras and Haiti, my father would pay the government a percentage of the proceeds from each successful operation. My father received this aid from the JLP.

My mother did not talk much about him when I asked. At times, I wished he had been there to mentor me like other fathers, but he was not. He had other plans to be in the streets than to be a part of my life. When I was in a terrible mood, I would sometimes turn my attention to my mother and give her a menacing look. In my mind, I was always wondering why my mother chose to raise her children with my father as the primary caretaker. A man who has never called me, sent me any gifts, or made any attempt to contact me in any way, shape, or form. Then I would pause and realize that I could not blame my mother because she was always there for me. If my father wanted to be accountable and responsible, he would have made efforts to be a part of my life.

THE TOOLS THAT MOLD ME

The rooster had already crowded for the morning. I knew this was my signal to hurry up and get out of bed before my grandfather discovered me sleeping late. Suppose I am ever found lying in bed beyond eight o'clock on the weekend. In that case, I would face harsh repercussions. I do not want to bring out the devil in my grandfather this early on a Saturday morning, so I would best get up and start my day by doing my regular tasks. The steps must be swept and mopped, the dishes from the previous night must be washed, and the big black tank must be refilled before the end of the day. Normally, I could sweep and mop the stairs quickly, but filling the sizeable black tank with water was always difficult. We do not have recreational water like in the United States. Our government gives the water we collect to drink as communal water.

I started my morning off by cleaning the steps first. Still, because it was the first summer weekend and neither my grandfather nor the elders were home, I opted to get water first to fill up the tank and do everything else afterward. I would have had the worst day of my life if I were ever caught. At times, my uncle would bring guests home and he expected the house to be presentable.

We walk miles with jugs on our heads to go catch water. The roadway where we catch water was constantly clogged with other neighborhood members. Some individuals would bring their donkey, others their automobile, others were standing by to take a bath, and others brought their pushcart with multiple jugs to get water. The wait was exceedingly lengthy, and we would sometimes get in trouble if we did not return home on time. Still, because my grandfather and the elders had gone to work and would not be home until the afternoon, sometimes we would skylark like to play cricket with the neighbors or pick mangos, eat sugar cane, and wait until it was our turn in line to get water.

"Watch your step, man, and don't step ova deh suh," my brother cried, alerting me to ringworms in a puddle near the pipe stand. I jumped over it and cautiously stepped down to crank the nozzle to turn on the pipe. If I ever stepped into ringworm water, I would acquire a fungal infection on my skin. Hesse's grandson, for example, his skin is covered with huge circles and painful rashes. No matter how often he attempted to cure them, they reappeared. Neither his mother nor father could afford to take him to the doctor. Some elders in the community advised him to apply Vaseline to the itches and bathe in aloe vera. However, no matter how often he washes in aloe vera and applies Vaseline to his skin, the rashes still appear on his body.

You see, Jamaicans are well known for their herbal remedies, and we believe drinking herbal tea can cure any illness. If a Jamaican guy sees Lazarus dying, he will advise him to sip some tea, and everything will be well. If you told an elder you were not feeling well, they would respond, "Oh, just drink some tea mon. It's just gas." Thank God Jamaicans were absent during Jesus' time because no miracles would be performed to honor God since Jamaican tea would heal everyone.

Carrying the jug of water on my head up the steep slopes was excruciatingly brutal. My hands were numb, my head was hurting from the bucket sitting on it for too long, and my feet were tired of walking. At times, I wished I could develop a system that would provide clean water to every household, rather than having everyone in the town travel to the lane to get water. My brother did it without hesitation. He was designed to carry big buckets of water up and down hills on his head. "Come on! Please hurry! Walk quicker, and do not let the water fall out!" screamed my brother as he held the barbed wire for me to cross the gully.

As I was carrying the water and cautiously racing to the barbed wire to make sure it did not spill, I began to think to myself whether life would be like a bucket of water on my head, with a lane full of people waiting to catch water, high hills, and gullies where someone waiting to hold the barbed wire and encouraging me not to let the water spill, and finally, counting each bucket while patiently waiting for the tank to be filled. If that is the case, I wanted it. I wanted patience, self-effort, humility, dignity, nobility, and integrity. If life is like a bucket of water on my head, it is the only life I want to be a part of.

The females in the household did not do as much as my brother and me. We usually received the most difficult tasks and the slightest sympathy. Although I despised cleaning and doing chores, my older brother often whined and complained more than I did. It did bother me, but I had no control over it, and refusing to cooperate would not help. What could I have done at the age of twelve anyway? Complaining would simply result in me being flagged. My brother once complained to my grandfather that he was the only one who usually did the dishes and pans. His grandfather beat him until he began bleeding.

After my brother's whipping, I was convinced he was dead. He was unable to move or even pull himself up off the ground. Now I understood what would happen if I opened my mouth in this house, so certainly I kept my mouth shut. Since seeing my grandfather's use of violence in hitting my brother, I always kept my mouth shut when a task was given to me. When addressing elders, I always addressed them as sir or ma'am to demonstrate respect or authority.

My grandfather has always been aggressive, but usually when he is drunk. When he was drunk, he would often start a fight or argue with my aunts and uncles and tell them to leave his house. This was one of the reasons why my mother did not live with him…because of his constant verbal abuse and threats. I remember one time he got so drunk he cursed my auntie out and called her a whore. The first time I recall seeing my grandfather drunk, I was shocked he acted out of character whenever he was under the influence of alcohol. His character changed and he transformed into a monster. There was something about his son Ryan that he did not like, and I still do not understand why. He picked more fights with him than anyone else. Knowing that Ryan had an anger issue did not help resolve the problem with my grandfather. On the other hand, Ryan was not like the others; he was much more of a go-getter and a more diligent worker than my other uncle, and, like my grandfather, he was a ladies' man; the difference between the two is that he understood how to keep a lady pleased and keep them coming back. They always appeared satisfied, but my grandfather did not know how to make a woman happy. Whenever he drank, he beat them, then called them provoking names. The sad thing about the women leaving him is they always left him for another man in the community who was less fortunate in life. At that moment, I knew that a woman was not looking for a man of courage but for peace, joy, and happiness.

One day, my Uncle Ryan urged us to clean up the house and fill the tank before my grandfather returned home. We did not clean as he instructed; instead, we picked mangos and visited the river. After he noticed that the steps were not swept and the house was not clean, he called my brother and me into the yard. He said, "You're a man, and if you don't know how to take care of your home take out the garbage, be humble and learn to take criticism and learn how to trim the grass; otherwise, the man you hire to trim the lawn and take out the garbage may end up mowing your wife's grass and emptying her trash can." What a remarkable speech. I put my hand on my chin and whispered to myself. "Being a man must be simple; what can be hard in taking out the trash, mopping the steps, and trimming the grass?" I remarked, finally hearing the solution of how to be a guy. I dab him up, hold my head high, puff my chest, and step off like a hit stepper. The next day I started mopping the house and taking out the trash because

I now knew I was no longer a boy, but a man.

My second uncle, Jordan, was the opposite; I had never seen him with a woman before, so he never gave too much advice on being a man. I had my doubts about his sexual orientation. I overheard him telling my brother one day that he never had a girlfriend because when he was younger, his brother dragged him to a papaya tree and urged him to whip out his penis and spank it on the tree to make it grow larger. But if the tree was chopped down, then his penis would shrink. He said that everyone stated it would work, and he thought the tree would grow forever, but when he returned the next day, the tree had been chopped down to the stump, and he said that his penis had never grown since. I assumed he was making an excuse because he wanted to date other sexes. He did not have the charisma or the demeanor to sweet-talk to the ladies like my Uncle Ryan. I was concerned about him since being gay in Jamaica was illegal and I did not want them to stone him to death. On the other hand, he had some clever ways about him. Jordan, you know, always had a deceptive attitude, and always outsmarted his peers. With his quick-thinking ability, he did manage to secure my grandfather a few tiling jobs. It is difficult for tilers to compete with everyone else on such a small island, but Jordan was a suave businessperson. He could persuade a rich guy out of his money and resell a pen to a CEO, which I found amusing because he could not talk a lady out of her panties.

Every day after work, he would count his earnings on the large pit in the backyard. "One hundred, two hundred, three hundred, four hundred." With a big grin, he would spin around in a circle and smile, then recount every dollar again. One day he went to a job and got paid plenty of money. The money was so much he could not carry it in his pants and had to pack some in his bag. I said, "Hey uncle, that's a lot of money you made today," He replied, "Sit, sit, sit down. Let me tell you summu, you see, there is no such thing as a lot of money, money can never be enough and never say this is a lot of money and promise me from now on that you will make more than this in your life that you won't be on a pit in the backyard counting it, but have someone in the bank doing it for you." I reacted cheerfully while roaring at the top of my lungs, "I guarantee it! I guarantee it! I swear to you, uncle!" He appeared satisfied with my reaction and slapped the money in my hands, saying, "Money is only enough when you start recognizing that it is enough." His statements left me speechless. Hearing him speak as if he were Mansa Musa motivated me.

I was curious how he got such an excellent education while Ryan could not read or write. Perhaps all eyes were on him since he was the family's baby. He worked harder to become a scholar. On the other hand, Ryan was a handy person who never saw the need to go to school like my uncle Jordan. Most people who attend college in the country wind up farming or working in a trade. Ryan was a tradesman with many talents, but reading a paragraph was not one of them. That is one more reason Grandfather despised him; perhaps he believed he disgraced the family by not properly pursuing his schooling.

It can be challenging to narrow down what it means to be manly and what constitutes the idea of a real guy. Today's politically correct culture frowns upon the traditionally masculine qualities of strength, honor, moderation, authority, and influence, all of which men were raised to want to possess. Men are told, in the same breath, that they should share their feelings, should stay connected with their emotions, and should be vulnerable. All these pieces of advice are meant to be taken together. Also, men are told that expressions of such feelings are either insufficient or, in the case of "negative" emotions, such as want, rage, and ambition, destructive.

In today's world, it is no longer possible for society to describe precisely what distinguishes a man from a boy. Now, society knowledge of what it means to be a man is pathetically weak. Young men cannot determine which of the several options would be the most beneficial to pursue and there is no one to whom young men may turn for guidance because most young men do not have any counselors available in their life. Because of our environment, males in today's culture are more despondent, confused, and enraged than they have ever been. This is directly related to the situation of the world. An epidemic of mental health issues, such as depression and worry, suicidal thoughts and behaviors, and needless violence, plague our civilization. Acts of unnecessary violence are among these issues. And, all the while, our culture laments the loss of "genuine males," asking aloud, "Where have all of them gone?"

Furthermore, young men are expected to critically consider how judgmental society can be concerning masculinity and critically examine themselves with alternative remedies to the challenges raised in political fiction of what features a guy must possess to be accepted as masculine, which in my opinion, is incorrect. What exactly is wrong with us as a generation? Crying and expressing one's emotions are seen as signs of weakness in men, who are expected to be strong and courageous at all times. But what happens when a man's faith crumbles, and he no longer has anything to lean on but his strength? Understanding this issue from the beginning is a promising idea, and the history of masculinity is a wonderful place to start because it is a sensitive subject to most. Examining the positive and bad aspects of traditional masculinity norms can help young men better grasp what it means to be a man.

The concept of masculinity in modern culture is indeed met with disapproval and unfair judgment by some. A woman looks to her husband to provide for the family. Thus, any sign of incompetence or weakness on his part might be seen as a direct threat to the stability of the home. Many people nowadays are understandably wary of conventional wisdom regarding what it means to be a man in modern society. Men in today's society are expected to suppress their feelings (save rage) and be tough at all times and these standards, often called "toxic masculinity," are harmful to males since achieving the ideals they represent is challenging and unpleasant. Because of this, most men are harmed by these expectations. They are bad for anyone who copes with aggressive male behavior, especially boys. It is unusual for people who critique masculinity to believe that men are fundamentally flawed. A set of expectations can be troublesome without negatively impacting the people subjected to those expectations. Isn't it possible to be manly in a way that benefits one's well-being? There is no justification for calling a man's standing as a man into question because he is a devoted father, an introverted, shy person, or a brave person. What makes a man a man is his nobility, character, and dignity. All these qualities are acceptable in a man; integrity, resilience, love, hope, self-discipline, empathy, adaptability, open-mindedness, gratitude, perseverance, generosity, self-awareness, and faithfulness.

In the grand tapestry of my life, I have uncovered a series of principles that serve as guiding stars, shaping the essence of who I am and the footprints I leave on the sands of time. At the heart of my journey lies integrity, a compass that points me towards the true north of self-discovery. Navigating the labyrinth of life's challenges, I have learned that maintaining my integrity is not just a commitment; it is a beacon that lights my path through the minefields of choices. With unwavering resolve, I walk the best path for myself, knowing that compromise is a shadow I shall never cast upon my commitment to integrity. But a life well-lived is not just about self; it is about extending a hand to others. The art of giving has become my currency of worthiness, a tender acknowledgment that in helping others, I find a richness that transcends material wealth. Providing for my family is not just a duty; it is a reflection of the generosity that flows from a heart unburdened by expectations.

In the dance between modesty and productivity, I have uncovered a delicate balance that hinges on the openness of my mind. Learning from the vast tapestry of humanity, regardless of age or background, has become my secret to both humility and achievement. By exposing my heart and head to the actions and perspectives of others, I have woven threads of connection and trust that bind the chapters of my life. And in the gallery of interpersonal connections, I have mastered the art of greeting with positivity. Direct eye contact, a firm handshake that echoes sincerity, a smile that radiates warmth, laughter that echoes camaraderie, and hugs that bridge distances—these are my tools. Every encounter is a chance to infuse the air with encouragement, to paint the canvas of connection with strokes of positivity. In the symphony of my existence, these principles are the notes that create a melody of purpose. Integrity, giving, openness, and positive greetings—they are the threads that weave the chapters of my story, each one contributing to the rich tapestry that defines the person I am and aspire to become.

We did not let the dogs into our house. The dogs were categorized as yard dogs and were always be kept outside. According to my grandfather, if the dogs are discovered wandering around the house or sleeping on the stairs, they would face the devil's wrath. He believed the dogs should be used for surveillance only around the home. One of our dogs, Milo, took a pleasure ride in the kitchen while my Aunt Shelia cooked. My grandfather happened to see Milo strolling in the kitchen and grabbed him by the neck with his bare hands and threw him into the gully. Being in the gully was a miserable experience. When it rained heavily in the highlands, the water became contaminated with rubbish, various bugs, and large pebbles. Tears welled up as I thought about Milo down in the gully. I wanted to rescue him, but I knew that being there was part of his punishment and that, if anyone tried to aid him, they would get beaten.

Ever since that day, we all started calling him the devil. The devil would use a cable length to tie the dogs to a lamp pole and flog the dog's numerous times. He would shout as he was flogging the dogs. "Didn't I tell you what would happen if I caught you in my house?" he roared as though he intended to murder the dog instead. When the other dogs saw what he had done, they were all frightened by him and would flee whenever they saw him coming. I used to believe the devil dwelt in hell, but now I know he lived with me, ate with me, and that day was flogging the dog right before me.

My grandfather was known in the community as a troublemaker. Because of his wicked intentions against others, his neighbors were all terrified of him. Our next-door neighbor causes an argument with my grandfather one day over his property line. My grandfather told him not to let his roster, cats, or dogs come onto his land because when they did, they usually pooped in the yard and sometimes stole from the kitchen. My next-door neighbor continued to let his roster, cats, and dogs out until, one day, my grandfather ended up catching a few of his cats and hanging them with a rope in a tree nearby the property line. After watching that, he never picked another argument with him. He did not let his animals walk on my grandfather's property again.

There was a rumor on the street that my grandmother had abandoned him for another guy in the United States. My grandmother left for the States one day and did not tell him, and I have heard that ever since he is not the same anymore. Once she left him, he exhibited terrible conduct against his family and friends and increased his drinking habits. He cursed his children daily, saying they were the main reason why my grandmother left him to find another man in the United States. He would yell at them stating "You're the main reason I cannot find another woman to settle down with and be happy." One day, he brought a woman to the house, introduced her to the family, and acted like Romeo had found Jasmine. I had never seen him grin before, and he greeted every one of his grandchildren and children with a kiss and embrace, saying, "This is my lovely rose in my garden; her name is Marcia," and as Marcia shook my hand, I grasped it tightly and looked her in the eyes. I wanted to shout, "Go away if you want peace, run far away if you desire happiness, far away, and never look back," Instead, I smiled and added, "Nice to meet you. My name is 'Shimpy' Clarke," my grandfather's nickname after hearing about my fights at school.

He took her into his room that day and made love to her. After she left, I never saw her again. He did not even talk about her to us no more. I always wonder what occurred between her and my grandfather. I wanted to ask my grandfather how she was doing. Still, I was afraid of his reaction, so I simply sat there, pretending that she would return one day so we could all see him happy or that she had found a better gardener to water her rose. My grandfather had been introducing us to all his roses for numerous years. I was thinking to myself now. "When will he remove the rose from the vase and put it in his garden?". However, due to his unhealthy drinking habit, which caused the explosion of domestic violence, he lacked the ability for any roses to flourish in his garden. That was when I noticed that happiness is like a butterfly in a garden. If you chase the butterfly, you will never catch it, but if you focus on the weeds and cleaning out the dry leaves in your garden, the butterfly will return one day and land on you.

He started to go to witch doctors for them to cast spells to entice my grandma to return to him and love him, which was ultimately unsuccessful.

Voodoo was traditionally practiced by most of our community's elders. Some claimed to have seen spirits and devils in the appearance of a rolling calf, also known as a "duppy bat" in other terms, spirits with unusual features. They would seek guidance from these spirits and, on occasion, compel the spirits to torture their adversaries or fulfill their will. Since doing voodoo and casting spells were the norm in my town, various prophets would visit us from all over the island merely to speak on behalf of the evil of witchcraft and that people should walk away from doing wickedness. However, the spells did not work. My grandma divorced him after leaving him for a white man in America. He did not discover they were no longer married because my uncle Jordan was the one that signed the divorce papers. My Grandmother did it for two reasons: she wanted to become a U.S. citizen to sponsor us and so we could move away from my grandfather's terrible domestic behaviors.

Agony is multifaceted, and sadly, the implications of such occurrences are not always limited to the time the traumatic experiences occurred. The sorrow induced by my horrific childhood experiences was a multidimensional item that brought me anguish. This is especially true for me because my parents and guardian were abusive when I was a child. The continual squabbling and arguing made my life a living hell, and I had to put up with-it day after day. Domestic violence can have a disastrous effect on your life if the person who is supposed to love and protect you fails to do so. Some may have been victims of physical abuse, which is the form of abuse that most people think of initially since it can be "seen" so quickly. Others may have been sexually abused. Others may have been subjected to emotional abuse as a child, a sort of mistreatment that is less commonly recognized but can be just as destructive. This mistreatment can be a victim's most challenging barrier to recovery.

If an abusive upbringing influenced a person's worldview and sense of who they are, it could be difficult to properly navigate life as an adult, regardless of the abuse they experienced as a child.

Every day brought new violence and an element of the unknown. Rules followed one day were rendered void and ineffective the next. Promises were not kept, and no attempt was made to make them suitable. My grandfather's expectations were always different, whether he was drunk or not. When he was sober, though, his expectations remained consistent. His temperament could swing significantly from one extreme to another in seconds, like a pendulum swinging back and forth. He was the happy and upbeat father one moment, then the authoritative figure who was strict and angry the next. As a result, even when everything was going well on the surface, I stayed on edge, waiting for the inevitable disaster to come. I started keeping track of the things that would set him off, and I made it a point to stay away from those triggers as much as possible. When I could not defend myself from my grandfather's fury, since I was the one who had provoked him to attack my older brother and me, I was left with feelings of inadequacy and guilt because I was the one who had prompted him to attack both of us. My grandfather occasionally took it out on his children to fulfill his rage.

It took me a long time to realize that he was venting his anger on us to feel some relief. He could be appeased most of the time with verbal and emotional abuse, which was sufficient. However, when he was under the influence of alcohol or was upset, his anger resulted in more physical abuse.

I undoubtedly had many questions regarding where my mother was, given everything was going on. Because my mother was residing in another state with my biological father and sister at the time, she was ignorant of where my brother and I were and what was going on. I did not have time to sit and feel wrong about the few slaps or burns I suffered on any particular day because I had to flee out of the yard, run down the street, wait until he was calm, and finish yelling before I could even consider feeling bad about it.

Growing up in an atmosphere where I was subjected to either physical or verbal abuse, I developed a habit of burying my feelings. I decided to keep a thoughts diary. I used it to document my emotions by writing songs and poems about how I felt then, the causes for those sentiments, and how I dealt with them. If I was communicating how I was feeling with someone for the first time, I always started with tremendous caution, taking small risks within my comfort zone. If the response was positive and encouraging, I let a little more of myself out. It took some time, but I have finally gathered a few close friends who value and recognize me for who I am. This was a time-consuming procedure. I began to be better at sharing myself by being more open to my classmates, and I quickly discovered that I was not the only one who was experiencing the same problems at home that I h

MY SPIRITUAL JOURNEY

At an early age, I learned that there are many ways to worship spiritually in Jamaica. These include Catholic Churches, New Testament Churches, Seven Days Adventist, Rastafarians, Maroon Town Worshippers, and many other churches that I cannot list because the list would go on and on. Everyone believes that their way of worship is the only way to heaven. Obeah is one of the spiritual practices some believers use, which can be employed to either heal or harm opponents. According to some researchers, Obeah's origins are linked to the Ashanti people of what is now Ghana and their practice of obayifo. These tactics were widely used in Jamaican slave resistance and revolution. Obeah men and women, also known as adept herbalists, are sought mostly for the treatment of physical, spiritual, and mental ailments and protection from hostile spiritual forces.

Growing up in school, I learned about the Pukumina, a Jamaican Revivalist tradition with more structured beliefs and practices than Obeah. This tradition is currently practiced in most major U.S. cities, with numerous churches and congregations. Despite many links between Jamaican Revivalist organizations and West African civilizations, outsiders are more likely than insiders to label Jamaican Revivalist groups as "African." Various Revivalist activities in Jamaica resemble religions from West Africa and Haiti. For example, each Revivalist spirit is said to have preferences for various foods, colors, and music.

The Pukumina ceremonial space consists of "ritual architecture" comprising a central pole to which Jamaicans have added a water basin for spirit channeling. Drumming and dancing induce trances and interaction between believers and spirits, providing divine healing or spiritual inspiration.

Some worshippers also identify as believers in Jesus Christ, which was a little confusing to me because they invoked the name of Jesus Christ for healing and power, despite their hearts being far from Him.

One day at school, one of my friends talked about his grandmother and how she was a witch doctor. He would walk around with his chest held high, shouting, "My grandmother is a witch doctor, so don't mess with me, or else she will turn you into a dog." Everyone feared him, including the teachers. When I first learned about witchcraft, I despised the practice of evildoers and the purpose of idolatry in serving the devil. I was unsure about establishing a closer relationship with God, and I began praying more than usual at the age of seven.

My friend Joseph had just lost his mother to a natural sickness, and I did not want to lose my mother. So, my prayers were intended for her. I prayed as they had taught me at Sunday school during devotion. "Dear Lord, God, please let my mother live for ten more years. Oh Lord, let her live to see 15 more years. Oh Lord, let her live to see 20 more years." Finally, I would pray to the Lord to allow her to live to see many more years. I did not know much about the creator, but I knew there was One. My prayers were short since I did not have many words to say at an early age. I did not know much about the Bible, but what I had learned in Sunday school regarding how Jesus died for my sins and that He would be coming back soon for the saved ones gave me reassurance. Still, I was open to giving my life to God and learning more about who He is and what He is capable of. Although my prayers were brief, I was receptive to giving God control of my life.

I have never stopped thinking that God chose me to be unique. I know He heard me, and I know He is listening to my needs. I always had a strong faith that God had favored me since birth because not one morning would pass without me giving thanks for another day, nor would I go to bed without praying— especially blessing the meal before I started eating and even when traveling back and forth to school. I would

always say a prayer of faith, guidance, and favor. I never thought of myself as Daniel or walking with the Spirit of Elijah. I am always humble, knowing that God has made me in His image to be a child of the light unto this world. At an early age, I confessed, "I am not my own and that I belong to Jesus Christ." This is the faith that guided me throughout my journey in life and led me to be baptized in the name of Jesus Christ and receive the gift of the Holy Spirit. Later, in my early twenties, I started to evangelize and preach the message of the gospel.

TELL ME SUMMU

Tell me summu!
Why is humankind at war?
Why is reality check so far?
Why does the penitentiary have so many Black men behind bars?
& Why do we quick to pick the matter out of our neighbor's eye, and
forget to pick the maggots out of our own scars?
Tell me summu!
Who gave them the right to take away our freedom?
Who owns the bombs and the steel guns?
Who is the man behind the real funds?
Who do we blame for the kid that was killed because the officer thought
he had a real gun?
Tell me summu!
What is righteousness?
What is faithfulness?
What is kindliness?
What is worthy in this world to lose and yet still be priceless?
Tell me summu!
How do you know what is a loss if you have never gained?
How do you expect a man to be a prophet if he was not ordained?
How do you expect the crop to spring if you have never watered the
grain?
How do you expect to be treated the same if you have never treated
others the same?
Tell me summu!
Where do we go now?
Where is the love that we should all bestow?
Where is the promise? Where is the vow?
And where is the love & dignity that we should all endow?
Now tell me summu?

The good thing about morning devotions at school is that the principal,
Mr. Romance, always has a Bible verse for the day and a motivational
speaker. One day, he announced that a unique guest visitor would join us
that day—Mr. Smith, the head commander of the Black River Police
Department. I had often heard my grandfather talk about Mr. Smith,
known to collaborate with the Dons in the community, supporting them
with money, drugs, and guns. Despite his seemingly good exterior, rumors
circulate that he was a bloody and deceitful person, involved in criminal

activities. To me, he was no different from the criminals he arrested.

Throughout the year, the small town of Black River has become overpopulated with deportees, drug trafficking, and some of Jamaica's most-wanted criminals. People's transformations to change their appearance were just money-making schemes. For instance, some pastors preached about God's words, but their actions never aligned with their preaching. I understand that, for some, appearance meant more than having a clean heart and a good conscience.

Mr. Smith addressed us, saying, "Children, life is a journey, so make the right choices. If you make good decisions, you can be successful like me. But if you waste precious time warming the bench in school, you will end up in my jail cell." As he spoke, I observed teachers cheering him on and applauding, even those familiar with his criminal activities. "Yes, keep on talking, Mr. Smith, it is so true. You are so right about these young kids. They are just wasting their time in school and taking education for granted when so many others are in their place right now," my teacher, Ms. Johnson, shouts as if she is waiting in line to cast her vote for Mr. Smith to be the next president.

Learning about corruption at an early age altered my outlook on life. Observing how others abuse public or organizational authority can negatively affect society. In Jamaica, crime has traditionally been considered one of the critical root causes of poverty. Police corruption in Jamaica has directly impacted the degradation of respect for the rule of law, the erosion of departmental discipline, and the harm done to police morale. The public's distrust of the Jamaican police is also a direct outcome of police corruption.

The amount of effort put into getting bribes and the overall number of payoffs made by criminal politicians and shooters are two factors that can be used to differentiate between levels of corruption. If conditions within a police agency permit corrupt acts, Jamaica's corruption level is deemed at its worst. This is the case when the level of corruption in Jamaica is at its highest.

Accepting bribes from persons involved in illicit activities like gambling, prostitution, underage drinking, and illegal drug use is law enforcement authorities' most common corrupt activity. Furthermore, this is the most common type of corrupt activity. The vast majority of police, though not all, believe that this type of dishonest behavior is not just benign but also of little concern to the broader public. As a result, they have an easy time explaining it.

Theft, collecting small gratuities, accepting kickbacks and other rewards, and fixing traffic citations are all examples of corrupt behavior. Corruption also includes dealing with criminals, accepting little gratuities, collecting bribes and similar "rewards," and getting small compensations. Accepting bribes from other law enforcement officials is another example of corrupt behavior.

Community standards, attitudes held by police chiefs, attitudes held by rank-and-file officers, police discretion, and actions taken by prosecutors and courts all contribute to corruption in the police force. Other elements contributing to the deterioration in the police force include: If the police chief is to be effective in combating corruption, he must have the authority to implement extensive systemic reforms and be well-versed in politics and administration. Speaking out, boosting the efficiency of internal affairs, strengthening inspections, ensuring that everyone in a position of responsibility is accountable, improving discretion, and decreasing corruption via training are all parts of a reform plan. These are just a few of the potential reform components.

SUMMER ON THE ISLAND

Without looking at a calendar, I could tell what day of the week it was and what month it is. As I listened to the church bell ring for Sunday school, the light, airy atmosphere brightened up the beautiful summer Sunday morning, filling my ears with the passion of joy and praise. Sunday school ran from 10:00 a.m. to 11:00 a.m. We would attend church service after Sunday school, ending at 3:00 p.m. We never had the chance to eat breakfast because we had to get up at 7:00 a.m. to bathe and fetch water before going to Sunday school. The church would offer us corned beef blended in butter with white bread in the morning. I overheard an old lady sitting under the big mango tree saying, "I would rather eat out of the trash can than this cheap nasty food." I nodded, then considered what the lady had said. I immediately changed my mind about eating the provided sandwich. I stepped into the church with a hungry stomach because it was difficult to digest.

I attended the New Testament Church; the pastor was my next-door neighbor, so I would always be on my best behavior and pay attention during service. After service, I would go home and have a worship session in my bedroom or outside on the balcony, then say a word of prayer for my mother and a brighter future. My mother and cousin would hear me worshiping and praying and mocking me. They even said I was stupid and did it to get attention, but I did not let their words bother me. I still pray consistently.

Every American dreamed of sitting on a hillside, staring at the lovely scenery, while eating a mango. People from all over the world come to visit the island as if it were heaven on Earth. When all we desired was to live their lives. We spent most of our summer picking mangoes, stealing sugar canes from people's lands, and playing marbles and cricket. Because Jamaica has a tropical environment, expect hot weather, high humidity, and tropical rain showers throughout the summer. Temperatures increase from June to November, with daily highs around 91 degrees Fahrenheit. This is the greatest time to visit Jamaica for a cheaper and more relaxing vacation. Even if rain and storms are a possibility, there is generally plenty of sunshine to go around.

Staying at home and not going to school was both a blessing and a curse. It was a luxury not to get up early every morning and travel in the dark to carry water. Still, waking up to another conflict or argument every day was a curse. My family never had tranquility. When we hosted a gathering, it was usually assumed there would be drama. Summer should be an excellent time to unwind and enjoy the warm breeze. I wish my summer had been spent in peace rather than war.

If you continued up the hillside for a bit farther, you would be able to see the beach in the distance. My house was around 45 minutes away from the ocean. I had trust and belief that simply staring at the gorgeous view of the beaches from a distance could help one generate excellent memories, especially when accompanied by a short 10-minute walk. My brother and I used to go for infrequent treks up the hillside, and while there, we would talk about our future hopes and dreams and how we saw our lives growing.

An early morning stroll down the sandy shoreline was the most incredible way to see the sun rise over the landscape. This should be done in the early morning hours. The waters have been carefully conserved, and there were opportunities to go snorkeling and view the thriving reefs just a short distance from the beach. The beach was remarkably peaceful, offering some of the best options for solitude anywhere in the world. This was especially true when you are out on the water, having fun, grilling fish, and roasting yams.

When my grandfather was not home, summer was the perfect season to play cricket, marbles, soccer, and hide and seek. They were some of the best times to bond because not just the kids, but also the seniors in the house came out to play. The game made an enormous difference and helped to relieve some of the stress in the house. We would play games from the afternoon until the sun went down.

LEARNING THE HISTORY OF JAMAICA

Let me share with you a tale of how delving into the rich history of the Caribbean, particularly Jamaica, has been a journey of discovery and awakening for me. Envision a vibrant island nation, a tapestry of towering mountains, lush rainforests, and sandy beaches kissed by coral reefs—a place pulsating with natural treasures from all corners of the Caribbean.

As we delve deeper into the heart of Jamaica, secrets unveil themselves: hidden waterfalls and sprawling forests, especially in the enchanting Parish of St. Elizabeth, rightfully hailed as the nation's breadbasket. It is a place where farming and agriculture thrive, weaving an essential part of the island's identity.

Yet, Jamaica's history is not just a picturesque landscape. It is a story of resilience and triumph over adversity, a narrative etched with tales of growth and perseverance. The island's motto, "Out of many one people," echoes through time, encapsulating the unity that defines Jamaica's identity.

But let us rewind the clock to the early days when the echoes of buccaneer pirates resonated through the Caribbean. Jamaica was their hub, a treasure trove where they invested in natural resources and brought enslaved people from West Africa to work on sugar cane plantations. Visit Alan Bamboo in St. Elizabeth, and you will still find remnants of those sugar cane plantations, a tangible link to Jamaica's past.

Port Royal, a historical port town, stands as a living museum, showcasing slave chains and weapons, testaments to the island's complex history. Yes, Jamaica is rich in natural beauty, but it has weathered storms— literal and metaphorical—through earthquakes, hurricanes, and periods of scarcity, fostering a spirit of resilience among its people.

I have witnessed hurricanes sweep the island, a formidable force demanding preparation and unity. Supermarkets stocked up, communities came together, and the true Jamaican spirit emerged in the aftermath. It is a spirit that mirrors the post-storm cleanup—a collective effort, a reminder that the nation stands as one in times of need.

Now, let us journey back even further to the time of the Arawak people, the Tainos, who first settled in what we now call Jamaica in the 17th century. They named it Xaymaca, "place of wood and water," a testament to the abundance they found. The Arawaks were known for their friendly and hardworking nature, thriving on the crops they planted and their prowess in fishing.

However, their peaceful existence was disrupted by the arrival of Christopher Columbus in 1494. In his quest for exploration, Columbus encountered the Arawaks and, initially considering them hostile, set his sights on claiming the island for Spain. The Arawaks resisted, but tragically, many were killed or injured during the encounter.

As we reflect on this journey, it becomes a poignant reminder that history is a tapestry woven with threads of triumph and tribulation, a narrative that shapes the identity of a people. Jamaica, with its resplendent beauty and intricate history, is not just a nation; it is a living, breathing story that continues to unfold, inviting us to explore, learn, and appreciate the rich tapestry of its past and present.

PERILOUS TIMES IN JAMAICA

Perilous times have come,
Violence and crime a mash up little jam dung,
Whooiee my brethren walking with a big gun,
And saying bwoy must dead and shot should fly through lungs.
In the street the crack they endorse,
Everyone flying high like they in first class,
but I don't need no weed or grass,
Cause The Most High God done tell me like jimmy cliff, many rivers I
must cross!

Following that, Christopher Columbus could set foot on the island and stake his claim to ownership. Admiral William Penn and General Robert Venables of the English Royal Navy successfully launched an assault on Jamaica that ended in the island's surrender on May 10, 1655. Following their defeat at the hands of the English, the Spaniards freed their slaves before fleeing to Cuba.

"Maroons" refers to the original set of enslaved people and subsequent generations of people descended from Jamaica. The buccaneers who eventually landed in Port Royal were reputed to be naturally curious during the early years of English rule in Jamaica. Curiosity defined these people's early years about everything around them. They were a very harsh and aggressive band of sea rovers noted for their irresponsibility and disregard for safety. They had begun their exploits on the Caribbean islands of Tortuga and Hispaniola, regarded as the birthplaces of the buccaneering tradition. They set out on their trek to Port Royal, bearing their gold, silver, and priceless stones.

Before this, Port Royal, Jamaica, was a tranquil tiny town with negligible impact on the world. After around a decade and a half of buccaneer rule, the city had become one of the "wealthiest and wickedest towns in the world." The reputation of the community grew with it over time. The operations of the buccaneers fueled this expansion of enslaved people throughout the country.

Henry Morgan was, without a doubt, the most successful buccaneer captain in history. He had a brief experience as a pirate before deciding to become a privateer. Morgan was well-known for his ruthless raids on Spanish ships and territories throughout the Caribbean. His exploits brought him a lot of attention. Because of his efforts, the Spaniards concentrated on securing their coasts, giving them little opportunity to invade Jamaica.

At the time, Jamaica was a Spanish colony, and the Spaniards were the first to change the country's name to what is now called Jamaica in 1507. The tremendous earthquake that struck Port Royal on June 7, 1692, was responsible for the city's destruction. Those Kingston residents who survived the quake and relocated to the city center departed the Port of Kingston. Port Royal began to come into its own as a critical naval outpost when it gained notoriety in the seventeenth century.

The Jamaican Constitution, adopted in 1962, is the country's most important legislation. It guarantees all Jamaican citizens the same liberty, rights, and advantages. The United States of America's Constitution represents sovereignty as a nation-state. It continues to serve as the foundation for the island's many legal systems and institutions. This is because the country's founders created the Constitution.

Jamaica obtained formal independence from the United Kingdom on August 6, 1962, after being under British colonial authority for over three hundred years. This incident marked the beginning of a transition that would eventually lead to the country's constitutional government. Even though it was the nation's first Constitution when it gained nominal independence, it was not the island's first legal structure. Instead, it was the nation's first Constitution when it became fully independent. Most individuals on the island, including myself, believe we live in slavery, notably mental enslavement and slavery induced by the constraints placed on us. They freed our ancestors from bondages and chains, but not their minds.

Picture a school where every lesson was a gateway to curiosity and wonder. For me, those gateways were Social Studies, Science, and History—three subjects that became not just academic pursuits but lifelong passions.

Social Studies, with its tales of diverse cultures and societies; Science, unlocking the secrets of the natural world; and History, narrating the stories of those who came before us, all left an indelible mark on my curious mind. Among the branches of Science, Astronomy held a particular fascination. The cosmos, with its celestial bodies and unexplored frontiers, beckoned me to gaze beyond our terrestrial confines. It sparked a dream, a goal that stretched beyond the confines of my classroom walls—I aspired to become the first Jamaican astronaut to venture into the vastness of space.

The thought of floating weightlessly among the stars, peering down at Earth from the cosmic abyss, fueled my imagination. It was not just a career goal; it was a dream woven into the fabric of my aspirations. I envisioned representing my homeland, Jamaica, among the celestial pioneers who dared to venture beyond our planet. Each lesson, whether it was deciphering historical events, understanding the intricacies of scientific phenomena, or exploring the stories of diverse cultures, was a steppingstone toward that cosmic dream. The classroom became a launchpad for my ambitions, and the textbooks were my star maps guiding me toward the uncharted territories of knowledge.

Beyond the academic realm, these subjects instilled in me a profound sense of connection to the world and the cosmos. It was not just about memorizing facts; it was about understanding our place in the grand tapestry of existence. So, as I pored over the pages of Social Studies, Science, and History, I was not just learning; I was embarking on a journey—one that would shape my understanding of the world and fuel a cosmic dream that transcended the boundaries of our planet. The classroom, with its lessons of the past and the mysteries of the universe, became the launching pad for a dream that reached for the stars.

CONNECTING THE DOTS THROUGH MUSIC AND POEMS

Street fighter, street fighter does not sleep at night,
Street fighter, street fighter bust their gun sometime,
Street fighter, street fight goes everywhere,
Street fighter! well I am a street fighter, and I do not care what people
say. Yes, I am a street fighter, and this is who I am.
Well, I am a street fighter with the knife. I am a street fighter with the
nine. I say your betta watch ya back when ya get out at night.
I am a real pimp guy. I ain't playing with no chick,
I am a hustler surrounded by thugs, no snitch.

In the quiet corners of my existence, a melody lingered—a soft hum that resonated within the depths of my soul. Little did I know that this melody held the key to unraveling the intricacies of my own identity. As the days unfolded, I found solace in the rhythmic cadence of words. It began with scribbles on worn-out notebooks, a collection of thoughts and emotions that sought expression. These musings evolved into verses, and verses, in turn, found harmony in the strings of my guitar.

Music became my refuge, an intimate conversation between the lines and the verses that danced through my mind. Each note and lyric became a dot waiting to be connected. The more I delved into the world of composition, the more precise the picture of my true self emerged. It was a revelation, a mosaic of experiences, emotions, and dreams woven into the fabric of my songs and poems.

Through the creative process, I discovered the power of vulnerability. My pen became an instrument of introspection, navigating the labyrinth of my thoughts and feelings. I unearthed fragments of my identity that had long been dormant with each composition. It was as if the music and poetry acted as a mirror, reflecting to me the intricate patterns of my existence.

The journey of connecting these artistic dots was transformative. It was not just about creating music and poems; it was about discovering the nuances of my being. The verses became a narrative, a story told in stanzas, weaving together the highs and lows of my journey. Each chord struck was a revelation, and every lyric penned was a step toward self-discovery.

The process was not always harmonious; there were moments of dissonance and echoes of unresolved emotions that found expression through the melodies. Yet, it was through these dissonances that the most profound connections were made. The music became a vessel for catharsis, a medium through which I could articulate the inexpressible.

As I shared my compositions with others, I realized the universality of the human experience. The dots I connected in my life resonated with others, creating a shared tapestry of emotions and stories. Through music and poetry, I found a language that transcended barriers, a means to connect with myself and those who resonated with the melodies of shared experiences.

Ultimately, what started as a solitary journey through verses and chords became a symphony of connection. Through music and poetry, I found my true identity and the profound joy of sharing that identity with the world. The dots connected, and the melody of my life played on, echoing the harmonies of a journey well-lived and well-shared.

I began authoring poems and rapping to express myself more. Writing songs had become one of my favorite talents; I would compose new music and have my classmates listen to the lyrics that flowed through my sensational mind. I began getting a lot more respect then because people saw I could do something useful: rapping, and all the girls liked my style and flow. I was starting to feel like Vybz Kartel. My rhyme was flawless, and my lyrics were tight. Now I was a part of this world because I had a talent people liked and respected.

Everything I did before failed. When I tried for cricket, the coach believed I did not swing the bat fast enough; when I tried out for volleyball, the coach claimed my shot was too soft and slow. On my third day of trying out for soccer, I was booted out of the draft. I attempted to do track and field, but the coach advised me to take my skills elsewhere because I would not fit in with the team. In primary school, I felt worthless, like a piece of stone that the builder would reject. My only desire was to be cool like my other friends and play on a team, but my abilities needed improvement. If my grandfather had just allowed me to play soccer, cricket, and do other sports with the other guys in the community, I could have improved my talents and made it onto one of the school teams, but instead, he said he was only protecting me from becoming a street rat and a gangster like my father. Instead, I was told to stay home, do house chores, and read my book. I told myself, "I need to start writing new songs to sing at school." My friends are always excited to hear my rhymes, and I am the only one at school who can rap. They would not mind if it sounded lame because no one understood how to write or rap or could contest me in battle rap. At school, this made me feel undefeated, like the last man standing waiting to be crowned with the belt of the championship.

"Me run this say no bwoy can test me,
Me leggo couple shot bend him up like the letter S,
No test me,
Me no sweet like nestle."

My rhymes were merciless and foreign, and I pushed myself to go beyond and over to write songs and poems that no one else could have imagined. You must be exceptional to be a dancehall/reggae community member. I was battle-rapping with other rappers in my town who were much older than me when I was eleven. Even though I never won the battles, the experience drew me in. Seeing how people respond to my music and lyrics has made me influential.

Embark on a journey into the vibrant world of Jamaican dancehall, where one artist reigns supreme—Vybz Kartel, the enigmatic Adijah Palmer. In the rhythmic heart of the Caribbean, Kartel carved his path as a music artist, songwriter, record producer, and entrepreneur, earning the moniker "World Boss."

Vybz Kartel's meteoric rise to folk-hero status in Jamaica is nothing short of legendary, marked by contentious songs and a mischievous public persona. Rolling Stone describes him as a provocateur who has consistently captivated the dancehall crowd and challenged the sensitivities of his critics. Introduced to the public by dancehall luminary Bounty Killer, Kartel quickly became a force to be reckoned with, not just in music but as a cultural icon.

His journey began in 2002, a year that saw the emergence of Kartel with an unparalleled string of hits. Stone Love, a renowned label, honored him as Deejay of the Year at their 30th-anniversary celebration, cementing his status as a dancehall powerhouse. Inspired by this recognition, Kartel embarked on a solo career, releasing his debut studio album, "Up 2 Da Time," in 2003—a resounding success that catapulted him to the forefront of the music scene.

However, amidst the accolades and acclaim, a darker chapter unfolds. Kartel's life takes a dramatic turn, culminating in a prison sentence for the tragic killing of Clive "Lizzard" Williams. The echoes of this event resonate beyond the dancehall beats, casting a shadow over the artist's legacy.

Yet, amid his triumphs and tribulations, a personal narrative emerges—a story entwined with my own experiences. Vybz Kartel, a favorite performer of all time, became a point of contention in my household. My mother, disapproving of his perceived lyrical content, urged me to turn away from his music and focus on more widely accepted talents.

It was a tale of conflicting perspectives, where the allure of Kartel's music clashed with familial concerns. In navigating this musical journey, I grappled with questions of identity, artistic expression, and societal expectations. As Kartel's beats pulsed through the narrative, my personal story unfolded—a tale woven into the complex tapestry of Jamaican dancehall, where the melodies of Vybz Kartel echo, not just in the music, but in the intricate nuances of my own life.

I remember when I was in kindergarten, when I was practicing for my graduation, and I was in the yard rehearsing my Spanish words for graduation.

"Uno, Dos, Tres, Cuatro, Cino," "shuuuuuuuuuut up! shuuuuut up! and stop saying nonsense". You are always acting foolish, but you are not, so do not make people believe you are stupid. Act as if you know what you're talking about. When I was called to the mic to perform at my graduation, I looked at my mother and the audience. I stutter and keep my head down until my teacher calls for another performer. "Why?" Why couldn't she see that I was trying to better myself and connect the links to figure out who I was? Instead, I was silenced because they were more concerned with other people's opinions than my family's self-assurance. Since then, I have learned not to trust the opinions of others. I have found my voice; I have learned to control my emotions, celebrate difficulties, distance myself from everything negative, become content with myself, and live without regrets.

Do you see? Happiness has always been present in my life. I just do not see it very often. When you stop looking for happiness outside of yourself and relying on others to make you happy, you will discover that you can rely on yourself as the key to mastering happiness and loving others. At this point, I realized that life is a sequence of random events and immutable decisions that I must deal with until I can make more changes. Music's incredible vibrations can have a significant impact on not just the mind but also the body. Listening to faster-paced music makes me feel more awake and boosts my ability to focus and concentrate. Listening to happy and cheerful music makes me more upbeat and excited about life. Because a slower tempo can calm my thoughts and muscles, it puts me at ease and lets me let go of the stress that has built up throughout the day. Using music to promote relaxation and reduce stress is a beautiful technique to achieve these objectives.

COMING TO AMERICA

My auntie told my mother privately that my grandma would support our trip to the United States. They murmured in the home because they did not want my grandfather to discover we were all departing for the United States. So, I was finally leaving this country and returning to the United States. Lord, I pray that the demons in this country leave me alone and that I can eat as much as I want and live the American dream. Going back and forth to the embassy was exhausting, especially after standing in line for hours. It was the longest line I had ever seen. I was exhausted after several hours. Finally, the representative called our name. My mother had taught us what to say to the agent the week before, so it was as simple as selling a story to a movie theater. We began to act differently after receiving our invitation and hearing that we had all been welcomed to America. Even the way we walk alters as though we are superior to others. Now I see why Jamaicans living abroad act superior to their fellow Jamaicans back home and act like gods or goddesses, claiming to be superior to everyone there when they return to Jamaica. They carry themselves as if they are operating at a higher level. While staring in the mirror, I thoroughly examine myself and my reflection. "This is it; this is your chance to make a difference. This is your chance to shine and show the world what you are capable of," I added.

Austinnnnn!!! Please come outside, my mother urged, destroying all my inspiring lectures. She sat me down and said, "We're going to America in a few days, and I don't want you to disgrace me or make me seem bad, so if you're thinking of going there to cause trouble, tell me now so I can avoid the problem of you being deported, and I'll leave you alone here."

I was the only member of the family that received counseling. Why do these people believe I will take over as Don in Fyyes Pen? I am neither a King Pin nor a bad Juvenile. It is either my personality, which no longer expresses itself, or Mass Hesse's grandson recently tried to offer me a rifle to fire. I am not sure why I am always the family's odd one out, but I know it will change one day, and I will show them that all the awful predictions they have made about my life will be proven false.

I told my friends I was going the next day when I got to school. It will be a sad day because they will be unable to hear me crack jokes or rap any longer. I was sure my professors would miss seeing me, especially because of my friendly demeanor. One of my greatest fears was adapting to a new situation and not establishing friends. I had some of the best friends in the world here, and I would not swap them for anything. Going to the airport on my last day in Jamaica brought tears. I cried dry tears because I was so delighted and could not feel my face. We are flying out the next day and staying with my grandmother. At the airport, we grabbed a few photos and discussed our plans. One of my ambitions was to work as an air traffic controller at an airport. It is always fascinating to watch planes take off and land. To me, watching it was therapeutic.

My first flight made me feel like I was finally making an impact. Things were going according to plan. I pondered whether I could fly away from everything and be at peace by myself while in the air, looking at the clouds as they passed by. Now I wish I had the wings of a dove; oh, how I would fly, fly, fly far away and find some serenity. We spent almost two hours in immigration after the plane landed, doing fingerprints, and taking photos. After immigration, I saw a woman greet us I had never seen before. Auntie Davis accompanied my grandma to the airport to pick us up. She was kind and pleased to see us arrive safely in the United States. My brother and I were stunned when she inquired what we wanted when she stopped at the corner store to get some drinks. We could not decide what to get, and I was still dreaming, so someone had to slap me awake "Please give me a Sunkist and a peanut snack," I finally said. I was pleased, and now I see the difference and the change. I did not have to believe that I was living to die anymore, but that I had a greater future ahead of me, that was worth living for.

It was not as difficult as I had thought to fit in at school. Everyone liked my accent and thought I was fantastic because I came from the island. People would always ask me to say something in Patois whenever I spoke, and I would oblige by saying "wah gwan mon" until I became bored.

APPRECI-HATE YOU

Jealousy & envy they call it,
But a dutty bad mind the Yaadie them call it.
Yute, you see ah foreign do not think say you and the Yankee them are the same.
They watch you work like a slave and end up taking the fame.
Then they would say me brethren, I appreciate you.
But we all know say the dutty badmind them appreci-hate you.
Red green and gold, Me say half of the story have never been told,
They sell out their pride for twelve piece a gold,
Why they so cold?
You nuh see say them renta dread yah do not have no soul.
They are doing the wrong things.
See the Black man there selling out the Black kings,
So, when you go a foreign, please do no bad things,
They say I want you do good, but not better than me, and if you rich they are supposed to be richer, and if you have a BMW, they are supposed to have a Telsa.
But do not worry me brethren, I appreciate you,
But we all know say the dutty badmind them appreci-hate you.

In the heart of my homeland, Jamaica echoes a national motto that resonates with unity: "Out of many, we are one." It is a phrase that encapsulates the spirit of a diverse nation coming together. However, as I journeyed to America, a land painted with promises and opportunities, I confronted perplexing realities.

In my Jamaican experience, significant discrimination and Black-on-Black crime were unfamiliar specters. The tapestry of Jamaican society, woven with a myriad of cultural threads, reflected harmony rather than discord. Yet, the American landscape presented a stark contrast that begged for understanding and exploration.

Questions lingered in my mind like the haunting refrain of an unsolved melody. Why did gang killings permeate communities? Why did African Americans harbor resentment towards immigrants striving for success, only to face blame when promotions came our way?

The narrative unfolded against a backdrop of complexity, where societal dynamics intertwined with individual struggles. As I sought answers, I delved into the undercurrents of race, identity, and the pursuit of the

American dream.

The issue of gang violence became a lens through which I viewed the fractures within society. It was not just about crime statistics; it was about understanding the roots of the systemic challenges that fueled the cycle of violence. Pursuing these answers became a personal journey where I navigated the intersectionality of race, poverty, and the pursuit of a better life.

The dichotomy of African Americans resenting hardworking immigrants held its layer of complexity. It was a narrative woven with threads of economic anxiety, fear of displacement, and the struggle for recognition in a society fraught with systemic challenges. Instead of being a sanctuary of opportunity, the workplace became a battleground of conflicting narratives.

As I grappled with these observations, I discovered that the answers were as intricate as the questions themselves. The American experience, a land of promise and potential, also harbored contradictions and disparities that shaped the narratives of its people.

"The Motto" is not just an exploration of disparities; it is a journey of comprehension, empathy, and the pursuit of mutual understanding. It is an attempt to unravel the enigma of societal complexities, all while holding onto the belief that, in the end, the motto "Out of many, we are one" can extend beyond borders and resonate as a shared aspiration for a more inclusive and harmonious society.

Observing how Jews and Hispanics live and rejoice together makes them stronger. I wish Black-on-Black had the same effect. The first time I was called "nigga" was by my African American classmates, and I did not like the word and the manner it was used in. I felt unappreciated and disrespected. He later tried to have bullied me in a class by saying to speak good English. I felt as if I was fighting against my own, yet I did not put up a spirit of retaliating; I ignored his ignorance and kept on learning. In English class, the teacher handed out the result from the state exam. I passed my exam with 94 percent, above the passing mark of 65 percent. He blatantly asked me, "How did you pass the exam when you barely spoke English?". I responded, "Isn't it a shame that I can barely speak standard American English, and you who were born here can and happen not to fail the language that you know the most?" He shut up and looked at me with shock, and he did not expect me to respond in the manner I did with a bold attitude of victory and a smile.

Many neighborhoods and businesses in the United States are still separated by race. The most severe offense was black-on-black. Black people are more prone than white people to murder one another. Hundreds of young people are killed daily over nonsense, and only a few small non-profits strive to fix the problem. I do not believe a coordinated national effort is happening to solve the obvious problem.

SHE IS AN ANGEL ON EARTH

She is an angel on earth but a witch in heaven,
Forgive me God but this witch is unpleasant,
Her love is like Facebook free to join, and it is open 24/7,
How are you twenty-four and your first child just turned eleven?
gurllllllll! You got me so sprung,
And even thou she got a man she is sexing the whole gang,
I said baby just love me once and forget your old man,
She said no baby once you are loving me you got to give me the whole
bank.
Gurllllll! Boii, stop maccin,
You ain't got nothing but a dime so stops acting,
And before you see my drawz I got to see your paper stacking,
And to get me in the groove bottles better be poppin.
Gurrrlll! You got a heart like an angel and wings like a dove,
She loves so many boii, that she did not even love,
As long as you got money, weed, good sex and you is a thug,
You can love that gurrl anytime even thou she is married and in love.

In the realm of firsts and newfound emotions, I experienced a transformative event that left me spellbound—the first time I fell in love. Picture this: it is like indulging in a scoop of ice cream, only to discover that it carries the unexpected but strangely delightful pizza flavor. The sweet and savory blend, a fusion of emotions, was as perplexing as it was enchanting.

As love's intoxicating aroma enveloped my senses, my brain grappled with the sheer intensity of happiness. It was as if every nerve ending in my body was savoring the unique blend of emotions, creating a symphony that echoed the joys of newfound connection. Each stolen glance and shared moment became the toppings on this extraordinary, albeit unconventional, love pizza.

Yet, as the story often goes, love is not always a seamless dance through happiness. The first heartbreak arrived like an unexpected storm, disrupting the serene landscape of my emotions. The ice cream with a pizza flavor suddenly turned bitter, leaving a taste of loss and melancholy.

The aftermath of that initial heartbreak was nothing short of madness. Emotions swirled like a storm within me, and my once-steady compass of reason became unhinged. It was as if the very fabric of my being had been unraveled, leaving behind a chaotic tapestry of emotions.

In the throes of heartbreak, I discovered the vulnerability that love brings. The pain was profound, but so was the growth. Each teardrop shed became a droplet of wisdom, and every sigh carried the weight of lessons learned. The journey from love's inception to heartbreak's aftermath was a rite of passage—a chapter in the book of life that forever altered the landscape of my emotions.

As I reflect on that first love, with its peculiar blend of joy and sorrow, I realize that it was more than just a fleeting emotion. It was a chapter in the grand story of my life—a story woven with the flavors of unexpected experiences and the ever-evolving tapestry of love and heartbreak. And so, the tale continues, with each subsequent chapter holding the promise of new flavors, new emotions, and the timeless echoes of love's transformative power.

In the labyrinth of love, I found myself navigating a terrain that seemed destined for the joyous union of marriage. Or so I thought. The breakup, an unexpected plot twist, cast shadows that lingered long after the echoes of love had faded.

From the day our paths diverged, sadness enveloped me like an unwelcome companion. Months turned into a relentless procession of melancholy that left an indelible impact on my spirit. The realization that she had moved on, and embarked on a journey with someone new, became a relentless storm, casting tempests upon the landscape of my emotions. The ache that engulfed me surpassed any pain I had ever known—a persistent, gnawing sensation that seemed intolerable. The specter of her presence with another haunted my thoughts, driving me to the brink of insanity. It was as if the fabric of my life was unraveling, leaving behind a tapestry of despair.

Depression, a silent intruder, stealthily crept into the recesses of my soul. The relentless hope I clung to, the belief that love would emerge from this emotional wreckage, now felt like a distant dream. In my desperate pursuit of love, I had placed all my bets on a relationship that was a mere illusion. The revelation that I was merely a friend in her eyes, a footnote in the story I had imagined would be our shared narrative, cut deeper than any blade. Once a beacon of affection, the woman of my dreams now stood as a shadowy figure—a puppeteer manipulating my feelings, playing with my heart as if it were a mere plaything.

Yet, in the depths of despair, a glimmer of resilience emerged. I refused to succumb entirely to the darkness that threatened to consume me. Instead, I embarked on a journey of self-discovery—a quest to overcome the ache and rebuild the shattered pieces of my soul.

I sought solace in the understanding that the key to my healing lay not in her but within me. The actions of another did not solely define the narrative of my life; it was a story I held the pen to. With each step, I reclaimed agency over my own destiny. It was not an easy journey, and the echoes of heartbreak lingered, but I made a pact with myself—to look ahead with better decisions and options. I immersed myself in an atmosphere of understanding love—not just for others but, crucially, for myself.

As time unfolded, the pain began to lose its grip. The woman who once held my heart hostage became a character in the chapters of my past. I discovered that resilience is not just about weathering the storm; it is about learning to dance in the rain. In the dance of self-love and understanding, I found the strength to emerge from the shadows, a phoenix rising from the ashes of heartbreak. The story, far from over, now carried the promise of new beginnings and a narrative shaped not by the ache of loss but by the triumph of resilience and self-love.

LOSING A PART OF ME

My entire life came crashing down. Everything I cared about was taken from me. On the inside, I am practically dead. I used to be such a cheerful, upbeat individual. My face was constantly bright with a smile. I was always a great sleeper. I cannot sleep now because I was shattered on the inside; I am always miserable; even if I appear joyful or smiling on the outside, I am tearing apart; I am still dead on the inside. It is not me. This irritates me. I do not know how to proceed with my life.

I am not sure how people survive such heartbreak! Primarily when it occurs unexpectedly. I needed to move on and put my feelings behind me so that I could begin to love again. I must learn to love again and avoid having my heart broken.

I built a barrier and began to love without emotion. This was done to conceal my genuine feelings. I promised myself that when the proper woman appeared, I would recognize her and marry her. I usually avoid pursuing more than one female at a time because it is inappropriate. A woman should not have to wonder if she is the only one, I like. She might feel less-than-extraordinary if she discovers others in her peripheral vision. And she would be justified in feeling that way. Therefore, I cannot treat her like that. I would expect the same from her end, and I would be disappointed if I discovered she was pursuing another guy while she was 'leading me on.' I have found that I can typically tell whether a girl is "the sort" who will pursue numerous people at once within a short time after meeting her.

After that, I had to recover from my first breakup. I decided to go on another date. This time, I took it gently and communicated effectively. I met her family and friends, and she was impressed and liked me for who I was. I was ultimately hers, and she was completely mine. For the first time, I lost a piece of myself.

Our first moment was built on chemistry and a strong bond—one of the most beautiful feelings I have ever experienced. For the first time, my thoughts had escaped the harshness and limitations of my family and were a serene place.

MY SILENT STORMS

"Who ate my bread, and whoever ate it has to repurchase it!" I overheard someone shouting early in the morning. Outside, I went to see who had eaten the bread. I am reliving the rumors of wars and horrifying domestic violence again. Still, this time it is my grandmother giving me the narrative rather than my grandfather. I am not sure what I did to offend my grandfather, but I am sure she hates me. But because she is always looking for a fight, I try not to bother her and even walk out of the way, so I do not hear what she is saying. There was never a time when there was no disagreement, or someone was getting into a fight. Bread, the television remote, gasoline money, mortgage cash, and even groceries became points of conflict. It is hard to believe we are arguing over food when everyone in the house makes a decent living.

I have had it with arguing and bickering. It forced me to mature vigorously in my heart and to grow apart from others. There have been times when I wished I had grown up in a more tranquil setting. What happened to King Solomon's saying, "Bring up a child in the way he should develop so that when he grows older, he will never deviate from it"? Where did the quote go? My family would sooner murder each other than build each other up from the ground up. There was always a problem in the house, from squabbling over who should pay the bills to who should eat each other's food. They even fight over who gets to sleep in late. The children in the house witnessed all of this until we began fighting. My cousin and I began to argue more frequently, and when we did, we would express malice to each other for weeks, if not months, as we had seen the elders do. Our issues would be solved if we did not communicate with one another. To avoid any talk, we walked far apart and never made eye contact.

I did not foresee living in America with my grandmother and family being so demanding. What happened to the American dream and the happy family we see on TV? Why are we unable to communicate with one another? My sorrow began at home, and these struggles have shaped who I am today. Throughout my life, I have had to overcome obstacles and endure failures. We are brought down when we face adversity and loss. As a result, I frequently feel unmotivated and even depressed due to these events. Regardless, the reality remains that we emerge from such experiences more muscular and more prepared to deal with inconvenient situations. Reflecting on it today, I can see how going through those terrible times shaped the person my partner and I have become. I would not be as wise, experienced, or compassionate to others if I had never been put down or if I had never gone through the challenging times, criticism, and failures that I have. I would not have the same regard for others.

I learn many valuable things as I attempt to find a way out of demanding situations. Because of these adversities, I got first-hand information and insight into what it is like to go through terrible times and how those times genuinely felt. I would not be able to enjoy eating some food if I had never had a bitter sensation in my mouth. Those who have demonstrated resilience in the face of hardship are more likely to keep their poise and modesty no matter what life throws at them, even when things are swimmingly. It is beginning to make sense to me that those who have been through adversity are more likely to sympathize with others who are currently going through hardship. They do not just dismiss others as inferior to themselves, nor do they discriminate against them based on dogmatic beliefs.

More important to me than the satisfaction of accomplishing a task is the education I acquired from my mistakes and the lessons I learned from them. Difficult circumstances force us out of our comfort zones and compel us to try new things. Living in a place with limited options forces us to be innovative and examine alternatives to traditional responses to challenges. I got the idea that I am being pushed to perform at a higher level than in the past while staying within the confines of what is permissible. This inspires me to be more conscious of resources, which I would ordinarily take for granted if not for this. I would take them for granted if it were not for this. I push myself to go above and beyond the usual methods when I need a challenge. The consequences are usually something exceptional and unexpected.

The more painful my experiences, the better I comprehend my flaws, genuine potential, and what I can accomplish. If I had not been assigned arduous work or placed in a constraining atmosphere, I would not have been able to accomplish as much as I have because I would not have pushed myself to my limitations. I have realized how critical it is to look for the countless other abilities and characteristics we possess. As a result of the difficulties and setbacks I have had in the past, I now have a stronger feeling of self-assurance. I am better equipped to face new obstacles in the future. As time passes, I become more accustomed to doing new things, devising backup plans in case something unexpected occurs, and participating in the most recent activities. My involvement in those fascinating experiences and arduous duties has inspired me to seek out more in the future. Those tough times, along with all the other excellent experiences and knowledge we obtained, have helped me become a more resilient and intellectual person than I was before. I have discovered that my risk-taking tolerance grows as I learn new things and acquire experience. Because of these diverse experiences, I now know how to embark on far more comprehensive adventures than the ones we have had up to this point. Finally, I could transcend my prior achievements and create larger and more in-depth schoolwork.

SEARCHING FOR THE UNCOMMON

When I was fifteen, I went out into the world in search of love, camaraderie, and confidence in the people I met but I could not find any of those things at home. I used to refer to one of my longstanding friends as Damion, the African prince. We attended the same high school, and it was there that I realized he was from Nigeria, so I gave him the great name African Prince as a nickname and to represent our friendship. Damion stated, "Man, if you're going to be on the block, you might as well do what we do," I knew deep down what he meant by joining the gang. Still, I initially ignored the request and just showed him love and went ahead with my business. Then, later during the week, I was riding the train going home, and as soon as I got to my stop, about five fives in red surrounded me and asked me if I had banged. I told them no, and they still ended up beating me up. I fought back but there were too many of them, and I could not fight anymore but just lay there on the sidewalk of East New York and took my whooping. Now I was out to get revenge, and my heart was bitter. Later I told Damion and the other guys what happened, and Damion asked me again. "You might as well do what we do if you're going to be on the block and be down with the gang."

I became involved in the activities of a crip gang when I was 16 years old. Joining the gang and becoming a member was the easiest but proving my loyalty and defending the neighbor was the hardest. Walking down the street in east New York, you could hear me from a mile yelling, "crip! Crippp!" Wherever I go, I would wear blue to represent  the gang I am purportedly a member of, even my bicycle was sprayed in blue. You should have trusted and believed I was present in the battle if my friends were involved since I have no reason not to. I never did anything without them, and they never left me out of anything; we were a family and a group of boys for the rest of our lives. During this time, I began to act more macho and gained the confidence to approach females. I try to get into the ladies' panties by smoothing them with my words, working confidently on what I say, and reducing my voice volume. Damion, another close friend in the gang, would regularly update me on this information about these females in the streets. Damion stated, "Now is not the time to go out looking for love. A whore and a rat are two categories of women who can be found on the street." He explained that a rat would go from home to house and sleep with everyone. In contrast, a whore would not sneak around from house to house. However, they would still sleep with everyone without shame, and he ended his parables by letting me know there is no love in dating these females. I was at a loss for what to do, and at that moment, I wondered to myself that the marijuana might be affecting him and that he should cease using it.

When I was 18 years old, I applied for and was awarded a scholarship to cover the expense of my postsecondary education. It was not easy to comprehend that I had been awarded a scholarship. Despite my inadequate communication skills, I was obliged to attend school, complete my homework, and return home. I do not know why the school, or the dean would select someone like me. The school did not even notice I was there most of the time because I did not make any trouble as the others did, and I also did not get into fights at school. Regardless of how much I gang bang, I did not bring the activity to school because school was the only ticket. I had to make a difference in my life and didn't want to be expelled. I am fully aware that I should not subject my mother to such humiliation, and the last thing I wanted her to learn about me is that I was a gang member. I did not want her to discover I was a gang member. I would be wrong to let my mother down because of her hard work; she deserves better. She was the only family member who worked and was responsible for all household finances. At the same time, my stepfather spent his days socializing with his cronies, smoking marijuana, and drinking beer. If my mother had discovered that I was gangbanging, she would have cried. The last thing I wanted to do was see my mother sad or in emotional misery. I do not want to add anything else to her plate because she already had a lot on her plate. After all, she had a lot going on.

When I discovered I was graduating from high school, I immediately informed my mother and everyone else in my community. I also announced it on social media. She hurried around Brooklyn, New York, jumping for pleasure and ecstasy as soon as she got the news, and she became even more thrilled than I was. A smile spread across her face as soon as she heard the news. I immediately began preparing for college and my graduation. I applied to several different schools and universities and was accepted to a few. The most important thing to me was getting a head start on my education and eventually earning a bachelor's degree to support my mother and the rest of my family. I had no reservations about attending a prominent educational institution. I would check the mail every day to see if I had been admitted, and when I found out that I had been accepted, I jumped for delight because Monroe College was my first choice for a school to attend.

Every day, I would check the mail to see if I had been accepted into another college. My mother gave me $200 to shop for a shirt and pants, so I rode the subway to the South Bronx, where I knew I could find the cheapest clothes, and began shopping. I went to the Arab store with only pants and a shirt in mind, but I could purchase a full suit for $150, and the tailor fitted the suit on me before purchasing it. I purchased it in the Bronx, right south of the housing complexes in the ghetto. The suit was not too inexpensive to wear; it was worth the money. The jacket and slacks were dark blue, but the top had a purple tinge. I was dressed to the nines for my graduation and looked so good. Now, I see why Tupac Shakur said all eyes were on me because I felt like a celebrity walking down the aisle of my graduation. I was decked and decked out, "I am the man and will continue to be the man," I told myself.

Damion "Watz Craccin Cuzzz," My longstanding friend, wished me serenity and informed me that our future is bright, and we have much to look forward to in the coming years. He delivered me a message of tranquility. One of the thoughts that raced through my mind at the time was that I needed to walk into my destiny, cease gang-banging, and let go of the old me. I shared my thoughts with him after graduation, and he wished me the best of luck throughout my journey in life. However, after some thought, we all concluded that the other gang members would regard it as disrespectful and read it as a hint that we were leaving them and that it would be viewed as an indication that we were abandoning them. I spent the autumn of my first year of college in New Rochelle, New York, where most people were 'blood,' delineating all blue and Crip territory in a predominantly blood area. I did not care, and I made it clear to everyone who I was and what I was banging. The rival gang members tilted their heads in my direction and stared at me, but none approached me.

Despite my banging, I made it a point to maintain my academic performance and attend class regularly. I did not believe wasting the scholarship money handed to me was proper. I also thought I should use the chance presented to me rather than destroy it. In other words, it was not appropriate for me to squander the funds. In my fourth semester, I began to reduce the amount of time I spent gang-ganging and focus more intently on my academic work and the responsibilities assigned to me by my lecturers. I solely obtaining A grades, reflecting this success. Due to my excellent academic performance, I started approaching the matter with the gang set I was part of, letting them know I no longer want to bang because I am doing well academically. Although some were fine with and understood it, others stared at me as if I were insane. I had the terrible sense that my life was in danger because leaving a gang after being initiated was considered taboo behavior. This was because leaving a gang was regarded as a sin. There is only one way in and one way out of this location. I was bicycling to Cypress Hills one day to see a friend who lived in one of the neighborhood housing units. My friend lived in one of the neighborhood housing units. When the gang members in Cypress Hills found out I was leaving, they condescendingly approached me to discourage me from going. On the same day that shots were fired in other city sections, a couple were fired in East New York. The gunfire had nothing to do with me.

Still, because someone else had been shot, the entire community remembered me and assumed I was involved. Although I had nothing to do with the shots fired, the entire community thought I was a victim. My mother was in tears when she called me and asked, "I heard you gag hitting, and you're a Crip. Is this the life you want to live?" My mum is a member of a gang. I was speechless and had no choice but to hang up because I could not think of anything else. Who could have told her I was banging? That was the only thing going through my mind at the time. The perpetrator was an older woman who lived opposite the street from us, just across from where we were. She was like the person who guarded the neighborhood; she kept an eye on everything and reported anything strange she saw; nothing escaped her attention.

My mother did not get much sleep that night, especially considering that most of the young kids involved in the gang-banging in our neighborhood died before they reached sixteen. She thought my Auntie Jasmine was correct when she informed me in Jamaica that I would not live to be seventeen because I would be incarcerated by then. My auntie Jasmine made such a prediction because she thought I would not make it alive. My mother then received a notice from the property owner requesting that she vacate the premises within thirty days since the owner intended to renovate the building. My mother was at a loss for what to do, so she contacted my auntie Shelia in Florida and asked if we could stay with her. My auntie Shelia consented to let us stay with her and agreed to look after us. I did not particularly appreciate living in Florida because of what happened with my grandma. I did not want to leave the area where all my friends lived because I did not want to leave them. I was miserable the entire trip to Florida since the car was so full that there was not enough room for us, and we were forced to squeeze into it.

They began telling us about the fighting in the family and how a rift forced everyone to go their ways as soon as we landed in Florida. They did not stop until they had finished their story. Hearing all these stories about people's arguments and rumors has made me long for my hometown of New York. I apologized but I could not take it anymore and had to give up. I was working to better myself, yet nothing appeared to change. My auntie eventually stopped talking to my mother and began giving her the silent treatment whenever she passed her. She did that every time they were in the same room. My aunt also told my uncle that my mother is irresponsible and is not responsible for paying any of the house bills because she is not liable for them. As a result, my mother was enraged and in emotional turmoil, and her heart was broken. My mother could have relocated but she decided to stay where she was because she believed that my aunt, out of the generosity of her heart, would have enabled us to wait until we were all ready to stand on our own two feet again.

I was lucky to find work as a houseman on Sanibel Island, where my duties included:

- Cleaning the premises.
- Collecting the trash.
- Aiding house cleaners with bedding changes.
- Repairing and maintaining air conditioning devices along with keeping the premises clean.

On Sanibel Island, I got the opportunity to work for the first time in my life. The cleaning of steps and doing the house chores finally paid off. Now I am doing it and getting paid as a houseman. In addition, I oversaw the repairing of various air conditioning systems and the remodeling of the plumbing infrastructure. Because it was my first job, I will always regard it as the start of my professional life, even though I have subsequently had numerous possibilities; and even though I wasn't dressed like most of my contemporaries who graduated college before me, I was humble enough to take it to balance some of my bills and some of my mother's expenses. I was incredibly grateful for this small start because I was aware of the beneficial impact this would have in the long run.

I felt valued because I worked hard to earn my money honestly and ethically. At this point in my life, I could not recall what it was like to be involved in gang operations. I was relieved I was not on duty to engage in drug trafficking on the street anymore. I could move on with my life without fear of the ramifications of my previous conduct. My new surroundings have given me a new perspective on life, so I no longer want to go with the flow of things that negatively impact my surroundings but continue seeking to improve myself. My new surroundings influenced my attitude and behavior. It had been more than a year, I had stopped gangbanging totally, and I had also begun to remove myself from the majority of my previous friendships. In addition, I quit smoking marijuana and started going to church daily, whereas before, I just went occasionally. In addition, I changed my phone number. I started wearing different attire, which resulted in my jeans no longer sagging on my buttocks. I wore other colors, including red and other colors my rivals were favorable of. When no one was available to give me a ride to church on Sundays, it was feasible that I could go there on my own time. I approached the pastor of the church I would be attending for two years and announced my wish to be baptized into the Christian faith. My mother was the most pleased with my decision to spend the remainder of my life serving God, and the rest of my family supported me.

My aunt Shelia has only recently begun to urge us to pay the rent, energy bills, and other property-related expenses. However, one day my mother texted my brother that the light bill was due, and it was $270; at the time, we both had problems paying it. My sister had been stubborn in her unwillingness to comply with my brother's repeated requests for a copy of the bill so that he could do his investigation. When my brother noticed the statement on her bedside table while she was at work, he confronted her one day. My sister was not in the house at the time. The bill came to fifty dollars. When my brother confronted her about it, she became agitated and blamed my siblings and me for everything going wrong. Everything started when my brother challenged her about it. After that, she kicked us out of her house, and I was forced to live in my car while my siblings went to live with my brother's girlfriend's parents. I ended up living in my car because she kicked us out of her house after that. After nine months since signing up for the military, the recruiter learned I was homeless and immediately sent me to a military boot camp in San Antonio, Texas, Lackland Air Force Base. He speeds up the process for me and brought me to the front of the line so that I could join the United States Air Force right away. I could not contain my joy at the time.

THE WIND DOES NOT BLOW IN THE WEST NO MORE

Sitting reminiscing asking God when will life change,
When will the sun stop rising,
When will stars stop coming out at night and when will the moon show
its face and stop hiding?
Then suddenly I heard He replied and said "son, the sun does not rise in
the west no more, and the wind does not blow in the east no more."
Lord, things remain the same,
I got a girl called life and she just bring me pain,
I am loving her real good but yet she just brings me game,
It is like life is a police officer, and this officer got me detained.
You see Lord, my dry moments are my real thoughts,
And I am humble enough to let you know my real thoughts like putting
a gun to my head,
And pull the trigger and buss a lead, cause even if I am dead...
He stopped me again and said, "son, just know the wind doesn't blow in
the west no more and the sun doesn't rise in the east no more."

I say, "I have to make a difference in this family and burn the cursed bridges of my ancestor generations." The pain of denial, the pain of being an outcast because I was different, the pain of not getting my opinionated view heard because no one cared for me. There were too many pains in my heart, and I refused to spread my pain to my children and my children's children. So, I made a covenant with God, asking Him to mold me, carve me, and use me in His Kingdom, and I will serve Him for the rest of my life if He only takes away the struggles of pain within my life. After graduating from George Westinghouse High School, I was fortunate enough to earn a college scholarship. After completing my first year of business administration, I began working as a facility manager at a small hotel. I did not want to go back to school. I wanted to learn more tactical skills rather than sitting in a classroom waiting to graduate and then not being able to find a job afterward like many of my friends. Something was missing. I started pondering and looking into myself; working for someone is a good start but I wanted to be my own boss one day. Working and going to school were outside my life goals. I wished to improve my tactical abilities. As a result, I enlisted in the United States Air Force. Finally, I was out of the house. I hoped my cousins and siblings would follow in my footsteps by attending college or joining the military, but they did not. My burning desire was to make a difference in the world. So, I ensured that I remained out of trouble and gave it my all at every chance. One of my friends I went to college with called me one day, saying he had just graduated and could not get an internship or a job, so he signed up for the military. I told my friend, are you crazy and insane? Why would you do that to yourself and throw your life away? He started to list all the positive and unique things about the military, not the negative stories you would hear as a civilian. I started investigating the opportunities and signed up with the Air Force recruiter. My first recruiter let me take the Armed Services Vocational Aptitude Battery (ASVAB). Still, it took me four months before I heard back from him. I took the initiative to drive two hours to see another recruiter, and I could take the ASVAB within two weeks and find out my ship-out date.

Basic training took a lot of work. I witnessed half of my flight leave and return home. I thought about stopping a few times but was hungry and determined to keep going. I could not march, shoot a weapon, or run for more than five minutes. I was blameless and had no idea what military service entailed. I began to think of the bucket of water on my head while jogging. I recalled the agony and strain of carrying the water up the hill. Still, the feeling of filling up the tank was satisfying, and that is how I was able to complete all of my runs and tasks on time, by remembering the bucket of water on my head.

I was overjoyed when I received my diploma. My mother, Uncle Ryan, and sister were the only family members that attended my graduation. It did not concern me that no other family members were present. Regardless, I was content. I began

posting images of myself in uniform on Facebook to make a positive impression on my Jamaican friends and family and demonstrate my success. I received numerous congratulations and prayers, making me feel like I had finally broken my family's curse of failing men. I wished my brother were there to laugh and share the memories with me. I hoped the news would spread quickly and reach my father so he would be aware of my accomplishments and the lofty goals I had set for myself.

We all received money for our time in training, so I was eager to check my balance after three and a half months of saving. I had 0.68 cents in my account when I called the bank to check. My savings had gone toward hair, nails, fast food, and other personal goods. I was stunned and speechless. Where did all my money go? My mother, like my sister, was dressed in the most recent designer. I politely inquired if my mother was using my card, to which she said, "I had bills to pay and wanted to buy a few things for this trip." My uncle Ryan told me that my mother and sister were frequently shopping with my card, so I know she did more than pay bills. This is my punishment for leaving my bank card with them to assist in paying the bills in the hopes that they would be merciful and save me some money. My friends were all heading to Whataburger that day while I was dining at Popeye's. My eyes welled up with tears, but they were dry ones. At the same moment, I was happy and sad.

THE STRENGHT OF A NOBLE MAN

On December 28, 2017, I married the woman of my dreams, someone I had a crush on for years and a friend since my first term in college. We met in 2012 on campus. Throughout the years of me traveling back and forth to Florida and New York, we never got to see each other much but we always stayed in touch on social media and by phone. While I was in the military, I decided to make a move and approach her to see if she was still on the market and open to chat. We chatted for a few months until she could visit Illinois and spend some days with me. We ended up getting married on December 28, 2017. Living alone, I had peace but getting married brought me happiness. When my wife moved, it was calm and paradise. Still, after a while, we started arguing over the smallest issues, which made me regret getting married.

As someone who has experienced both the wedding and honeymoon phases of marriage, I can say unequivocally that they are both fantastic experiences. However, once the honeymoon period had worn off and I begin sharing a home with the woman I called my wife, dealing with the adjustments that come with marriage were not easy. It was beneficial to have someone to rely on, spend time with, and share experiences with, regardless of whether things were going well. This held us both when things were going well and when they were not. Marriage had the potential to be an immensely wonderful experience. Still, it also had the potential to be quite stressful and demanding. Joy, contentment, a lighthearted connection, and passion were once defining characteristics of my marriage union; however, the communication, listening, comprehending, negotiating, fighting, and self-sacrifice required in a relationship frequently felt like a much heavier burden than what once were the defining characteristics of our marriage. The most significant periods in my life always come with some struggle. My wife and I have had to confront some of these problems together at various points in our marriage.

One of the difficulties that my wife and I had was the revelation of limitations, which occur after marriage. She and I tended to exert control over specific aspects of certain situations; nevertheless, neither of us could accept that we were not always in control of everything. Many people value their single lives highly because they believe they still have complete control over their lives even though they are unmarried. This false sense of understanding is evident in the setting of a marital relationship.

Being single, on the other hand, provides you with complete control over what you do, when you do it, and how much money you spend as a direct result of the activities you engage in. Marriage is nothing like that. It can be viewed as the union of two distinct kingdoms, with one of the kingdoms eventually clashing with the other; in my case, my domain was involved.

To clarify, it is incorrect to claim that once we marry, we go from being the ones in command to being the ones who are dominated. The most fundamental difference is that we went from total control to far less of it. I have less authority since the decisions now more directly than ever impact another person and, as a result, necessitate the involvement of that other person. For us, the result was we are more inclined to make bad decisions.

But why did our marriage have to begin on such a rough path? Because nothing in life compares to the sense of having no control over the events unfolding around you. Vertigo is a common side effect of losing control; its severity is not always proportional to how much power is lost. Giving up control may be paying such a great price to me that the marriage effort will be avoided, abandoned after acceptance, or emptied of all its beauty due to the demand that one person has complete control over everything. This is because the requirement for one person to have absolute power over everything necessitates one person has full control over nothing.

One of our marriage's most critical challenges was that we had to work hard to establish trust in one another and guarantee that trust was not betrayed. Sadly, our marriage was littered with broken trust several times, and trust is difficult to reestablish. This occurred before I left for a deployment. She traveled down from New York to begin living with me after we had moved in together. Many people find it difficult to trust someone when their trust has been destroyed, especially if the person who violated their trust was their partner; I was that person. Many people find it difficult to trust someone again after having their confidence broken. Some people can move on swiftly, forgiving and forgetting their lover almost immediately after discovering they have been unfaithful. However, if you continue acting as if the event never happened and ignored it, you will remember everything and feel your life has been flipped upside down. Even if it has been several years since your partner has broken your trust for whatever reason, there is still a potential that it will happen again. Participating in counseling sessions is beneficial in this situation. My spouse and I must both gain a better understanding of the issue that is generating misery. Confronting the issue is something both of us must do to move forward with fixing whatever is wrong and forgetting the grief that comes with it.

In the labyrinth of relationships, the tale of my first marriage unfolds—a narrative marred by misunderstandings and complexities, a tapestry woven with threads of uncertainty. Yet, within the intricate design of this union, I discovered unexpected wellsprings of hope, joy, and an enduring blessing named Micah. The early chapters of my marriage were marked by a dance of miscommunications, a symphony of conflicting expectations. The once-clear path of understanding became entangled, obscured by the fog of differing perspectives. The complexities seemed insurmountable, threatening to cast a shadow over our once joyfully exchanged vows.

Amid this discord, a beacon of hope emerged—a tiny heartbeat that echoed within the cocoon of my wife's womb. The news of impending parenthood introduced a transformative element into our narrative. Micah, our soon-to-be son, became a symbol of new life and a harbinger of strength and hope. As the days turned into months, the anticipation of Micah's arrival became a lighthouse guiding us through the stormy seas of marital challenges. His imminent presence inspired a shared commitment to weather the difficulties and discover the joy within our union.

The moment Micah entered the world, his cries resonated not just in the hospital room but within the chambers of my heart. His tiny fingers, a testament to the miracle of life, carried with them an unspoken promise—a promise of love, resilience, and the potential for newfound beginnings. As I held Micah in my arms, a profound sense of responsibility and purpose washed over me. He was not just a witness to our struggles but a catalyst for transformation. In his innocence, I found the strength to be brave, to face the complexities of my first marriage with newfound courage.

With his infectious laughter and curious eyes, Micah became a source of unbridled joy—a reminder that life, despite its challenges, is a gift to be cherished. His presence became a constant, a North Star guiding me through the uncharted waters of fatherhood and marriage. In the journey with Micah, I discovered that blessings often emerge from the crucible of adversity. His existence became the bridge that reconnected fractured bonds, an embodiment of hope that compelled us to rewrite the narrative of our marriage. While the complexities of my first marriage persist in the chapters already written, Micah's presence has infused the storyline with hope, resilience, and an unwavering love that transcends misunderstandings. In the symphony of our lives, he stands as a melody of joy, a testament to the transformative power of parenthood and the courage found within the embrace of family.

Despite going through difficult periods as a married couple, we also had many happy days together. For example, we discussed, set objectives, and participated in enjoyable local activities. My ex-wife and I found out we were expecting a child about two months before the start of my deployment. That revelation filled me with excitement, serenity, and hope that my wife and I could have a great marriage now that we had a kid to raise together. We may now pay attention to the child rather than vent our anger on one another. During my deployment, communication challenges were heartbreaking and were not working out. Although I did my best to assist her from afar throughout her pregnancy, I had the idea that I was not doing enough to meet her requirements. At this point, I realized it was hopeless; if we cannot keep open lines of communication, there is no use in sticking together. After I returned from my deployment, I witnessed my kid's birth, and then six months later my wife filed for divorce. I was relieved that we were splitting up because it gave me peace, but it bothered me that my child would never get to know both of his parents.

In the tapestry of my tumultuous journey with my ex-wife, there was a moment, a singular chapter, which stood as a testament to the resilience of hope and the strength that emerges in the face of adversity. It was a moment that unfolded in the labor and delivery room, where the cacophony of our struggles faded, and the raw, unfiltered beauty of life took center stage.

Despite the complexities that strained our relationship, the impending arrival of our child became a beacon of purpose—a shared hope that transcended the discord. Months of misunderstandings and disagreements seemed to dissipate in the face of the imminent miracle that awaited us. As the day of delivery approached, a palpable tension lingered in the air. However, amid the uncertainty, an unspoken agreement arose. For the first time in months, my ex-wife and I found ourselves joining hands in prayer. The prayers were not for reconciliation or the mending of our fractured bond but for a safe delivery, for the well-being of the life about to enter the world.

The hospital became a temporary sanctuary, a space where the echoes of our disagreements faded into the background. Days turned into nights, and I found myself immersed in a surreal existence where time seemed to stand still. The only rhythm was the heartbeat of life growing within her. In those relentless days, I became a constant presence at her side. I did not leave the hospital—did not have time to shower or rest. The only brief intermissions were the dashes to grab sustenance, a hasty refueling to continue the marathon of anticipation.

Then came the moment that suspended the universe in a breathless pause. A call, urgent and expectant, shattered the routine. It was her—my ex-wife—requesting that I bring her aunt home. Simultaneously, she revealed that the birth of our child was imminent, unfolding in the delicate dance between minutes and seconds. With adrenaline coursing through my veins, I leaped into my car, the tires screeching as I raced against time. The roads blurred into a mosaic of lights and shadows, every intersection a hurdle to conquer. The urgency of the moment eclipsed the troubles that had defined our recent past.

In the delivery room, as I witnessed the arrival of our son, a profound transformation occurred. The cries of a newborn wove a melody that drowned out the echoes of our disagreements. In that moment, I felt a surge of strength and purpose—a renewed commitment to navigate the complexities of co-parenting with grace and resilience. The birth room became a crucible of emotions—joy, relief, and an unspoken acknowledgment that life's fragility demanded a truce in our differences. In the cry of that newborn, I found a reason to continue the fight—not against each other but for the well-being and happiness of the life we had brought into the world.

The birth of my son became a chapter of redemption—a turning point, where the discord of the past gave way to a shared responsibility and an unspoken promise to nurture and protect the precious life we had created. In that sacred space, hope rekindled, and purpose found new meaning in the fragile, yet resilient, bond of parenthood.

IT TAKES A LOT TO MAKE A MAN FROWN

When people see that your mad, they are happy cause they want to bring
you down,
Have you ever wondered why children are so unbound?
Think about it, if they fight today by the end of the day they smiling &
still play in the playground.
Adults are not the same, we tense to fight a lot because of confusion &
as human beings we are easily distracted,
But only if we can only be as humble as a child and see that everything is
Worthwhile and to be able to love each other with a joyful smile, then we
be at our highest self in our highest prime,
So, before you start your day say a prayer and crack a smile and never
allow someone else to take away your joy.

You see war is always won by love. Rather than battling fire with fire, why not spread love? When the enemy brings battle, I bring peace, and when the enemy sets traps, I am overcome by God's joy.

I stumbled upon a profound lesson, one etched into the very fabric of my being. It's a story that unfolds like a gentle breeze, carrying with it the wisdom of understanding why it takes a lot for a man to frown and the heavy toll of staying ensnared in anger, blind to the opportunities that dance in the periphery when one's mindset clings stubbornly to a singular perspective.

The lesson began in the crucible of personal challenges when life seemed to conspire against me. Every road I walked bore the weight of adversity, and the skies above were painted with hues of uncertainty. During these moments, I discovered the resilience embedded within the human spirit, the inherent strength that allows a man to weather storms and resist the pull of a frown.

I observed the intricate dance of emotions within, realizing that it takes far more energy to summon a frown than to let the lightness of a smile grace one's countenance. A frown, I discovered, is a heavyweight emotion burdened with the gravity of negativity. To wear it requires a conscious effort, a deliberate choice to embrace the shadows when light is but a thought away. However, the crux of the lesson lay not just in understanding the weight of a frown but in unraveling the knots of anger that bind the soul. Anger, I learned, is a formidable captor, locking the heart in a relentless grip that stifles joy and blurs the vision of the opportunities dancing on the periphery.

As I navigated the labyrinth of my emotions, I realized that anger, when clung to, is a lens that distorts reality. It narrows the field of vision, leaving one blind to the myriad possibilities that await just beyond the tunnel of discontent. Opportunities, like elusive sprites, flit away when one's gaze is fixed on a single, irate perspective.

The turning point came when I decided to unshackle myself from the heavy burdens of frowns and anger. It was a conscious choice to embrace a mindset that saw life not through a narrow keyhole but through the expansive lens of possibilities. In doing so, I discovered a reservoir of untapped opportunities that awaited my gaze.

The narrative of my life transformed as I learned the invaluable lesson that it takes more muscles to frown than to smile, and it takes far more from the soul to harbor anger than to release it. The decision to broaden my perspective became the key that unlocked doors I had not known existed.

So, as I share this story, it carries with it the wisdom of a lesson learned—a testament to the resilience that allows a man to smile in the face of adversity and the liberating power of releasing anger to embrace a world of boundless opportunities. It is a narrative woven with threads of introspection. This testimony invites others to cast off the heavy burdens and walk, with a lightness of heart, into the waiting embrace of countless possibilities.

GOD FAVORED ME

I was the shining armor and the superstar within my unit. Email me if you want your pay fixed and have a quick turnaround with speed and accuracy. I was winning awards and accomplishing goals. I won the Airman of the Quarter award for Air Mobility Command two times back-to-back, five times Airman of the Quarter in my unit, and two times Airman of the Year, along with many others. I got coined by general officers and senior leaders. I made rank on my first-time testing, and I was promoted ahead of most of my peers.

In 2018, when I was deployed to a masked data location, this deployment altered my life and my outlook on the future path I want to follow. The United States wastes far too much money waging unnecessary wars and uses far too many resources for far too little cause and was not pleased seeing some of the reports of the after-effects the guys would do down range. After a few weeks into my deployment, I began to feel less and less compelled to continue serving my nation and more and more motivated to get out of the military once my term was over. At the time of my deployment, I was expecting my first child, Micah.

SAINT LOUIS ZOO
EXIT
The He

I CAN'T GO NO MORE

I cannot go no more because I will not make it,
My flesh is weak, and my mind cannot take it,
I try to stomp off the chain of curse but seems like stomping it will not
break it,
"Just give up and go back" the flesh said, but my soul keeps on whispering
"Austin, you can make it."
Because there is a prayer in my heart!
Singing sweet chorus throughout the war,
Saying the flesh is weak! weak! weak! but my soul is stronger than a two-
edged sword that is very sharp.
There it goes again, when you think it is all over it just begin, darkness,
obstacles, and tribulation of evil men.
We are not only wrestling against flesh and blood but against principalities,
against powers, against perilous times to the end.
But God strengthen us today,
For us to overcome the obstacles that is in our way,
if we should lose faith and disobey,
Send your angels to kneel with us while we pray.
Because there is a prayer in our heart!
singing sweet chorus throughout the war,
Saying the flesh is weak! weak! weak! but our soul is stronger than a two-
edged sword that is very sharp.

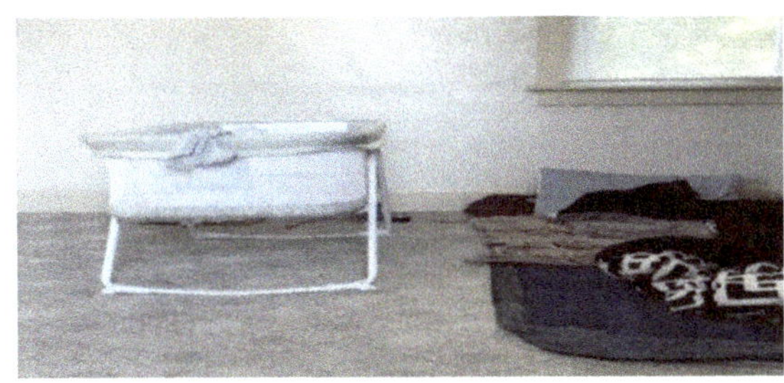

After getting divorced from my ex-wife, I moved out of our shared house and into an apartment with just one bedroom that fit comfortably within my financial constraints. The one-bedroom old house was very cramped; the carpet had a foul odor, and the windows were broken. I had to use an additional blanket during the winter because the air was so chilly. Bugs and insects were crawling all over me and my son's bodies when we were sleeping. The shower was inoperable and chronically blocked. Because there is dirt in the sink and bugs crawl out whenever the water is turned on, neither my son nor I can take a good shower in this house. Because the kitchen was so cramped, I could only prepare one meal at a time on the stove, and there was only one place besides the one bedroom for eating.

This brings back memories of an experience in which I had to share a bedroom with six other people. However, this time it was just my six-month-old son and me. I was not sleeping on the sponge-like before; instead, I was using a blow-up bed from Walmart that would only stay inflated for two hours before deflating completely, which caused me to miss the sponge.

Before tending to my son's nursing requirements, I would begin each day by getting up, reading from my Bible, and praying aloud before placing the Bible at the head of his bassinet. I would always make sure to have a portable speaker nearby to play some gospel music or listen to the Bible being read aloud. This chapter in my life served as the environment for God to break down the walls I had built up around myself due to the pride I had harbored in my heart without giving Him the honor due to Him as Lord.

I was so incredibly proud of being in the military, winning so many accolades, and becoming recognized for my service that I would sometimes forget to pray and skip attending church altogether. Even though times were tough, and we did not have much space to run around and play, we still managed to make some great and unforgettable memories together, such as going to the nearby park and walking around the block to show him the birds and throwing stones in the nearby lake.

VICTORY IS A SOUND OF HOPE

In the quiet moments of dawn, as the first rays of sunlight gently caressed the neighborhood, I found myself captivated by a daily ritual that unfolded like a sacred symphony. Living next door, there was a woman of unwavering faith, a silent beacon of hope whose presence became a source of inspiration for me. Every morning, just before I embarked on the day's journey to work, I would witness a scene that transcended the ordinary. This woman of God, name unknown to me but whose spirit spoke volumes, stood on the sidewalk with a shofar cradled in her hands. As the world around us stirred from its slumber, she would lift the shofar to her lips, and the hauntingly beautiful sound would reverberate through the stillness of the early morning air.

At first, I was merely an observer, a passerby in the intricate tapestry of her devotion. But with each passing day, I began to sense a deeper connection to this daily ritual. It was not just the melodic notes of the shofar that echoed in the air; it was the profound message they carried. This was more than a routine—it was a proclamation, a declaration of victory over unseen battles.

The woman's dedication became a silent sermon, a reminder etched in soundwaves that victory had already been won. As I stood on the threshold of a new day, the recurring image of her faithful act became a symbol of hope, a divine assurance that I needed to stand firm in my faith. This was no mere coincidence; it was a sign, a whisper from the divine orchestrator of the universe. The consistency of her presence  and the resounding echoes of the shofar became my daily anthem of encouragement. In those early morning moments, I found solace in the belief that the sounds of freedom, of victory, were already permeating the atmosphere.

The symphony of the shofar became a conduit for joy and happiness, a proclamation that transcended the limitations of time and space. Though her name remained a mystery to me, the woman's faith spoke a universal language—one that resonated with the core of my being. In her simple yet profound act, I discovered the power of faith to transcend the mundane and usher in a sense of triumph. As I stepped into the challenges of the day, the sounds of the shofar lingered in my heart, a melodic reminder that victory was not a distant goal but a present reality, waiting to unfold in the chapters of my life.

HAPPINESS IS A DIRECTION, NOT A PLACE

In the canvas of my life, if you were to take a closer look, you would find the strokes of hardship and the vibrant hues of hope. It is a tale that echoes the profound truth that happiness is not a destination; it is a direction, a journey woven through the fabric of resilience and optimism. The chapters of my story unfolded against a backdrop of challenges—twists and turns that could have easily cast shadows of despair. Yet, in each hardship, I discovered a wellspring of hope, an unwavering belief that there was always light waiting at the end of the tunnel.

Much like an unpredictable journey, life presented me with its fair share of storms. In those tempests, I sought not just a refuge but the strength to navigate through. The realization dawned that happiness was not a place I needed to find; it was a direction I chose to face, regardless of the circumstances.

One defining moment was the recognition that my outlook and perspective held the power to shape my experience. Happiness was not contingent upon reaching a predetermined destination but rather on the choices I made, the mindset I embraced. It was a revelation that transformed my journey from a mere series of events into a deliberate quest for joy and fulfillment. Amidst the challenges, I found solace in small victories and moments of gratitude. These were the  beacons of hope that illuminated my path. The realization that happiness was not waiting for me at some distant point but was an integral part of the journey itself brought a profound shift in my approach to life.

As I embraced this philosophy, the narrative of my life underwent a transformation. The shadows of adversity became the contrasting backdrop that made the hues of joy and hope even more vivid. Happiness became a compass guiding me through the twists and turns, an ever-present companion on the journey. It was not about glossing over difficulties but acknowledging them as part of the intricate tapestry of life. The journey, with all its ups and downs, became a story worth telling—a testament to the resilience that comes from understanding that happiness is not elusive; it's a constant, an ever-present force waiting to be recognized.

So, if you were to peer into my life, you would find a collection of experiences and a narrative that celebrates the direction of happiness. It is a story that whispers, in every page and every chapter, that hope is not a distant concept but a flame that flickers within, lighting the way forward. In the journey, I discovered the true essence of happiness—a companion, a guide, and a faithful co-traveler through the wondrous tapestry of life.

Because of the countless obligations and commitments that come with daily life, my life is usually highly hectic. Because I often juggle multiple duties simultaneously, I frequently find myself moving quickly and concerned with preparing for the next move. On the other hand, I encourage you to go at a slower speed so that you can concentrate on what you are doing and why you are doing it. It is critical to keep meticulous track of the outcomes of your actions. Even if it does not matter what other people say or think of you, you must be aware of how you affect the world. My son, my family, the things I enjoy the most, such as my work as a computer scientist and cyber security researcher and developer, and the people around me who support me by giving back and serving Christ, are the pillars on which I have built my life.

Furthermore, my church has been an essential part of my spiritual formation. The ideals I hold dear have served as the foundation upon which I have built my life. At this stage in my life, I am now looking for a better, brighter tomorrow, hoping to discover new opportunities for growth by making the world a better place. I make it a point to reflect on the truly important things to me, constantly weighing the benefits and drawbacks of the people in my inner circle and always looking for a better tomorrow. The key to happiness is enjoying your good fortune and the trials that allow you to triumph over life's unavoidable obstacles so that you can live your life to a whole degree of possibilities.

In the silent corridors of unresolved emotions, I stumbled upon a story, not of bitterness, but of redemption—a narrative that unfolded in the tender moments of forgiveness, prayer, and the unyielding belief in the transformative power of hope.

The tale begins in the shadowy recesses of my heart, where the weight of unresolved conflicts with my grandmother and grandfather cast long shadows over the years. Hurtful words and misunderstandings had etched lines on our family canvas, creating chasms that seemed insurmountable. But in the quiet moments of reflection, I found a glimmer of light—a flicker of hope that whispered, "It's never too late to mend."

Armed with courage, I embarked on a journey of forgiveness. It was not a swift leap but a gradual, intentional step toward healing. I realized that holding onto the past was a heavy burden that shackled not only them but me as well. The remedy, I discovered, lay in the balm of forgiveness—a salve that had the power to soothe wounds and resurrect fractured bonds.

Prayer became my silent companion in this journey of reconciliation. I sought solace in the sacred spaces of my faith, laying bare my pain, regrets, and hopes before a higher power. In those moments of communion, I found strength, not just for myself but also to extend a hand of understanding and compassion toward those who had once seemed distant.

The pivotal moment came when I decided to bridge the gap with words—words of encouragement, empathy, and a shared commitment to do better. I approached my grandmother and grandfather with a heart softened by forgiveness, expressing not just my own desire for healing but a sincere wish for our collective restoration. As I encouraged them to embrace hope and strive for better days, a subtle transformation began. Walls that had stood for years started to crumble, revealing humanity beneath the layers of hurt. I realized that much like me, they carried burdens of their own, and the remedy was not just in my forgiveness but in our collective willingness to change and grow.

Together, we embarked on a journey of rebuilding, each day offering a new opportunity to mend what was broken. It was not a linear progression, and setbacks occurred, but the commitment to never give up on hope became our guiding star. Through shared laughter, tears, and moments of vulnerability, we found a renewed sense of family—a tapestry rewoven with threads of forgiveness, understanding, and relentless hope.

In the end, this story is not just about the remedy I found for forgiveness; it is a testament to the resilience of the human spirit. It is a narrative that underscores the transformative power of extending grace, of fervent prayer, and of never losing sight of the hope that has the strength to mend even the most fractured bonds.

I AM NO LONGER A STRANGER ANYMORE

I am no longer a stranger in the church,
I am no longer in the street cursing God asking Him what life is worth,
One day He sent His Spirit to rescue me,
and from that day on, I am not a stranger in the church but a stranger in the street.
Frustration and anger I used knock without getting an answer,
Ignorance and cluelessness make me a tyrant monster.
However, I became humble as a servant to the redeemer, and He said,
"let no man despise thy youth but be thou an example of the believers".
Things I used to do; I do no more.
Places I used to go; I go no more.
So, when I read my Bible from Genesis to Revelation, He answers my supplication, and said, "go preach the gospel in EVERY nation."
Lord gives me the strength today,
To overcome the obstacles that is in my way,
If I should lose my faith and be disobey,
Send your angels to guard & protect and kneel with me while I pray.

I cried while drafting this poem, and my first time performing it in church left me nervous. However, I knew it was the truth—a testament that I am now a saved and new creature in Christ with no plans of turning back into the world of sin. I have evolved from Shimpy, the oppressive, monstrous adolescent who lacked an appreciation for the value of life. Address me as Austin, the appellation my mother gave me at birth, and as a Child of God.

At this point in my life, I am no longer in the service and am considered a United States Air Force veteran, having served for six years. I then worked remotely as a Senior Security Systems Engineer for Centene Corporation and as a Senior Software System Development Project Manager for USTRANCOM at Scott Air Force Base, IL. I serve as a spokesperson for diversity, ethics, and inclusion at the Global Center for Cyber-Security Conference and as a senior instructor at Grade

Potential Tutoring. Additionally, I preach the word of God online and coach others. Micah has shifted my priorities; I now find love in a different language and am delighted to call him my own. I began planning my transition from the military by completing my undergraduate and graduate degrees and obtaining additional certificates in Information Technology and Cyber Security. I purchased a large two-story house with a spacious backyard so my son could play and have enough room for all the fun activities he never had while I stayed in an old house. At the end of my contract, I gained many additional skills, including servant leadership, professional development, and career progression, which later prepared me for my civilian career.

In the tapestry of my academic and professional journey, I have woven a narrative adorned with degrees and certificates—an Associate of Science in  Finance and Accounting, a Bachelor of Arts in Business Administration, a Master of Science in Engineering Management emphasizing System Engineering, a coveted project management certificate from Cornell University, and the pinnacle, a Ph.D. in Computer Science. An Honor roll grad with Omega Nu Lambda, Security certificates, including CISM, OSCP, PMP, CASP+, CompTIA CySA+, CompTIA Security+ ce, and CompTIA Network+ ce, stand as sentinels to my commitment to excellence. Amidst these accolades, I also find fulfillment as a minister in my church.

However, life's narrative is a symphony that harmonizes triumphs and tribulations. The crescendo of my academic achievements was poignant when my mother received an eviction notice, a dissonant chord in our family's harmony. The property owner cited the dire need for roof repair and the removal of mold within 90 days. A hurricane's wrath had compounded the damages, surpassing the property owner's insurance reach.

News of the impending displacement weighed heavily on my heart, igniting a determination to transform this discordant note into a melody of hope. Fueled by a desire to provide my mother with a stable home, I embarked on the arduous yet rewarding journey of securing a home loan. Miraculously, approval came in the form of a half-million-dollar loan—a lifeline that promised a new chapter.

In a selfless gesture, I entrusted my mother with the reins of the house-hunting expedition. Guided by a skilled realtor, she ventured to find not just a house but a haven, a place where dreams could flourish. The joy that emanated when she discovered her perfect abode was a testament to the transformative power of resilience and hope. Within the swift rhythm of 24 hours, the chosen house was under contract, a testament to the synchronicity of our aspirations. The subsequent 30 days marked the culmination of this journey—a new home purchased; a refuge secured amidst life's uncertainties.

This tale is not just a narrative of academic accomplishments but a testament to the resilience that blooms even in the face of adversity. It is a story that underscores the notion that education and success, while invaluable, find true purpose when woven into the fabric of compassion and familial love. In the echoes of my journey, I see not only the melodies of achievement but the harmonies of hope and the triumph of securing a haven for my mother—a testament to the transformative power of love and determination.

My journey's story is marked by resilience and triumph against the odds. In the tapestry of my family's history, I stand as the pioneer—a trailblazer who dared to traverse uncharted territories. A story of service to the US military unfolds a narrative etched with sacrifice and commitment. But this tale does not end there. I pivot to academia, breaking new ground as the

first in my family to wield the mantle of a Ph.D. in Computer Science. The echoes of change resound—reverberating through the corridors of tradition. I am the architect of my narrative, the first to pivot and start anew. In the eyes of my aunt and grandmother, I become the embodiment of transformation. No longer the perceived foolish boy of yesteryears, I stand as living proof that adversities can be transcended and judgments can be shattered.

Each step forward is a testament to the triumph over preconceived notions and societal expectations. As I pass a mirror, the reflection staring back is more than a mere image—it reflects love, happiness, joy, and a profound sense of peace. The echoes of my journey resonate, and the values I hold dear are not just acquired; they are earned through the crucible of life's struggles.

"I have found love, happiness, joy, peace…and more and value," I declare to the mirror, acknowledging the depth of my journey. Yet, I am acutely aware that the trials harmonize this symphony of success endured, the challenges overcome, and the resilience forged through adversity. It is a story of personal triumph and a testament to the transformative power of embracing life's struggles and finding joy in the journey.

Love emerged as the unassuming hero, a force that not only fought my battles but also revealed a profound truth—that every soul is a unique melody in the symphony of existence, each cherished by a divine hand. The journey began in the crucible of personal struggles, where life's battles raged like tempests, threatening to extinguish the flickering flames of hope. In those trying moments, I discovered that love, a force often underestimated, possessed the resilience to withstand the fiercest storms.

Love became my armor, a shield that deflected the arrows of bitterness and resentment. It was not a grandiose gesture but a quiet, unwavering commitment to understanding, compassion, and empathy. With love as my guiding star, I navigated through the tumultuous seas of human emotions, seeking not to conquer but to connect. As I traversed the landscapes of experience and maturity, a profound realization unfolded—the uniqueness of each individual. Like a kaleidoscope, humanity revealed itself in myriad hues, each person a mosaic of experiences, dreams, and quirks. The once-blurred lines of judgment became clear, and I started to see that every soul carried a sacred uniqueness, a fingerprint of the divine.

In the tapestry of relationships, I embraced the diversity of personalities, recognizing that every idiosyncrasy was a stroke in the masterpiece of creation. The abrasive edges of judgment softened, making room for the vibrant colors of acceptance and appreciation. I started to understand that God, in His infinite wisdom, had woven a rich tapestry where every thread was deliberate and every hue intentional. With this newfound understanding,

I embarked on a journey of cherishing people for who they were, not who I expected them to be. The battles I fought were no longer against others but within the confines of my own prejudices. Love, the silent teacher, urged me to celebrate differences and cherish the beauty of diversity and as far as my relationship with my dad, I forgive him and accept him for who he is and help him financially when I can.

As the chapters of life unfolded, I realized that love not only wins' battles but also reshapes the narrative of our shared humanity. Each person, with their unique story, became a source of inspiration and a reminder of the boundless creativity of the Creator. I witnessed the transformative power of love, breaking down walls and fostering connections that transcended the superficial boundaries of appearance, culture, or belief. And so, in the pages of my book, love stands as the protagonist—an unwavering force that not only conquered personal battles but also illuminated the path to a deeper understanding of the divine masterpiece called humanity. It is a narrative that celebrates the uniqueness of every soul, recognizing that in the tapestry of life, love is the thread that stitches us all together.

CLOSING REMARKS

The essence of what it means to be a strong, noble man in today's society is woven into the fabric of challenges, character, and the undaunted resilience that shapes a man's destiny. The hurdles faced were not merely obstacles; they were poignant lessons, intricate chisels molding the image of a man destined to leave an indelible mark on his children and peers. The struggles, oh, they were undeniably real. They carved deep furrows into the landscape of existence, etching a story of endurance and fortitude. Yet, what emerged as more real, more tangible than the trials themselves, was the unwavering fight for joy—a relentless pursuit that transcended the somber notes of hardship.

In the crucible of life's challenges, character emerged as the linchpin, determining the trajectory of this man's fate. The choices made, the resilience exhibited, and the grace under fire became the brushstrokes painting a portrait of strength and nobility. It is a portrayal that extends beyond the individual, resonating as a legacy passed down to children and echoed in the respect of peers. The journey recounted within these pages is not a mere chronicle of struggles; it is a testament to the transformative power of challenges, the crucible where the mettle of a man is tested and refined. The scars borne are not blemishes but badges of honor, each telling a story of overcoming, of choosing joy in the face of adversity.

As the curtain falls on this chapter, let it be a reminder that obstacles are not roadblocks but steppingstones, each contributing to the shaping of a man—a man who, despite the tempests, stood tall with resilience, embodying the noble virtues that transcend time. In the tapestry of life, the struggles may fade into the background, but the fight for joy remains etched in the foreground—a resounding anthem that declares the triumphant spirit of a man who embraced the challenges, navigated the storms, and emerged not just unbroken but strengthened. May this story resonate not as a conclusion but as an invitation—an invitation to continue the fight for joy, for strength, and for the enduring legacy of noble manhood in the ever-evolving narrative of life.

As we conclude this journey through the pages of my book, I sincerely hope you found both enjoyment and a treasure trove of life objectives within its chapters. Allow me to glimpse the guiding principles that have shaped my perspective, which are rooted in a personal mantra that steers the course of my existence. My life's creed has never been about amassing material wealth; instead, it has centered on the richness found within the realms of hope and an unwavering faith in God. These intangible treasures have been my compass, directing me toward a life dedicated to extracting the utmost from each day, embracing the best within others, and contributing to the fortification of humanity's collective spirit. Life, as we know it, was never promised to be a canvas of perfection. Instead, it unfolds as a tapestry of challenges meticulously woven to sculpt and mold us into the ideal men and women God envisioned. It is a narrative of growth, resilience, and a continuous journey towards becoming the embodiment of the divine calling placed upon us.

In closing, let the words of Joshua 1:9 resonate as a timeless beacon of strength: "Have I not commanded you? Be strong and courageous. Do not be afraid; do not be discouraged, for the Lord your God will be with you wherever you go." May this verse echo in your heart as you navigate the intricacies of your journey, finding strength, courage, and solace in the divine presence that accompanies you.

Thank you for joining me on this expedition. May your path be illuminated with the wisdom gleaned from life's challenges, and may you continue to build and strengthen the tapestry of your humanity.